How to Build Storage Solutions

A DIY Guide to Building Custom Cabinets, Drawers, and Organizing Solutions for Your Home Workshop

James D. Parker

Table of Contents

Introduction

Have you ever looked around your home or workshop and felt overwhelmed by the clutter? Perhaps you've spent countless hours searching for the perfect storage solution, only to find mass-produced options that don't quite fit your space or meet your specific needs? Or maybe you've been shocked by the high cost of custom cabinetry and storage systems, wondering if there might be a better way? These are common challenges that can transform our living and working spaces into sources of daily frustration, limit our productivity, and even discourage us from pursuing our creative projects.

I've walked this path before. There was a time when I believed that creating custom storage solutions was a skill reserved for professional woodworkers, requiring years of experience and specialized tools. The prospect of building cabinets, constructing perfectly fitting drawers, or designing organized storage systems seemed intimidating and beyond my capabilities. However, I discovered that mastering the art of building storage solutions is not only achievable but deeply rewarding, opening up a world of possibilities for transforming any space. This realization changed not just how I approached woodworking, but my entire perspective on creating functional, beautiful spaces.

Imagine confidently designing and building storage solutions that perfectly match your needs, skillfully crafting drawers that glide smoothly, and creating cabinets that maximize every inch of available space – all through your own craftsmanship. Picture walking into a perfectly organized workshop where every tool has its place, or enjoying a clutter-free home with custom-built storage that seamlessly blends with your décor. Through "DIY Wood Storage Projects," you'll develop the skills and knowledge to make this vision your reality.

This comprehensive guide delivers professional woodworking techniques, design principles, and clear, step-by-step instructions for creating durable and functional storage solutions. Whether you're a beginner hoping to build your first basic box or an intermediate woodworker ready to tackle complex cabinet systems, this book will elevate your abilities from simple projects to sophisticated storage solutions.

In these pages, we'll explore:
- Essential woodworking skills for successful storage projects
- Understanding wood properties and selecting the right materials
- Professional techniques for precise measuring and marking
- Mastering fundamental joinery methods for strong construction

- Creating perfectly fitting drawers and doors
- Design principles for maximizing space efficiency
- Step-by-step guidance for building various storage solutions
- Expert strategies for hardware installation and adjustment
- Detailed finishing techniques for lasting beauty
- Advanced troubleshooting methods for common challenges

By investing in this guide, you're not just purchasing a book — you're gaining the ability to become your own custom cabinet maker, transform any space with personalized storage solutions, and save thousands on professional installations. Instead of settling for off-the-shelf storage that never quite works, you'll experience the satisfaction of creating exactly what you need.

Why continue struggling with inadequate storage and organization when you can build custom solutions perfectly tailored to your space? Dive into this guide now and learn how to design, build, and perfect your own storage projects. Are you ready to embark on this woodworking journey that combines practical skills, creative design, and precise craftsmanship? Let's begin this rewarding adventure together and discover the secrets to creating beautiful, functional storage solutions, one project at a time.

PART I
GETTING STARTED

Chapter 1
Understanding Wood and Materials

Selecting the Right Wood for Storage Projects

Before diving into specific wood selection, it's essential to understand that woods fall into two main categories: hardwoods and softwoods. Despite their names, these categories don't strictly correlate with wood hardness - balsa, for example, is technically a hardwood but is extremely soft. Instead, the classification relates to the trees' reproductive structures and leaf patterns.

Hardwoods generally come from deciduous trees (those that lose their leaves seasonally) and include:
- Oak (both red and white varieties)
- Maple (hard and soft)
- Cherry
- Walnut
- Birch
- Mahogany

Softwoods come from coniferous trees (evergreens) and include:
- Pine
- Cedar
- Fir
- Spruce

Key Factors in Wood Selection

When selecting wood for storage projects, consider these critical factors:

1. Project Requirements
   - Load-bearing capacity needed
   - Exposure to moisture
   - Visual prominence of the piece
   - Budget constraints
   - Expected wear and tear

2. Wood Properties
   - Dimensional stability
   - Hardness (measured on the Janka scale)
   - Grain pattern and appearance
   - Moisture resistance
   - Cost per board foot
   - Local availability

Selection Process

Let's break down the wood selection process into actionable steps:

1. Project Analysis
   - Determine the project's primary purpose (e.g., workshop storage, kitchen cabinets)
   - List environmental factors (humidity, temperature variations)
   - Establish budget parameters
   - Consider aesthetic requirements

2. Wood Property Assessment
   - Check wood hardness ratings
   - Evaluate dimensional stability
   - Assess grain characteristics
   - Review moisture resistance
   - Compare cost factors

3. Practical Considerations
   - Local availability
   - Tools required for working with the wood
   - Finishing requirements
   - Seasonal movement expectations

Operational Sequence for Wood Selection

1. Initial Assessment
- Measure the space where the storage solution will be installed
- Calculate the required material quantities
- Document environmental conditions (humidity, temperature variations)
- List any specific requirements (load-bearing capacity, moisture resistance)

2. Budget Calculation
- Determine total project budget
- Research current wood prices in your area
- Calculate cost per board foot for different options
- Include additional materials (hardware, finishes, etc.)

3. Material Evaluation
- Visit local lumber suppliers
- Inspect available wood options
- Check for:
* Straightness and warping
* Moisture content (use a moisture meter)
* Visible defects
* Grain pattern and consistency
* Color variations

4. Sample Testing (if possible)
- Request or purchase small samples
- Test finishing techniques
- Evaluate workability
- Check compatibility with planned joinery methods

5. Final Selection and Purchase
- Choose primary and secondary woods
- Select specific boards
- Inspect each piece for:
* Straightness
* Twist
* Cup
* Bow
- Arrange for proper transport and storage

Best Practices for Wood Selection

1. Acclimation
- Always allow wood to acclimate to your workshop environment for at least 1-2 weeks
- Store flat with proper stickers for air circulation
- Monitor moisture content during acclimation

2. Grain Matching
- Select boards with complementary grain patterns
- Plan cuts to maintain grain consistency

- Consider grain direction for structural integrity

3. Cost Optimization
  - Use premium woods for visible components
  - Consider secondary woods for hidden elements
  - Utilize plywood where appropriate
  - Calculate efficient cutting layouts to minimize waste

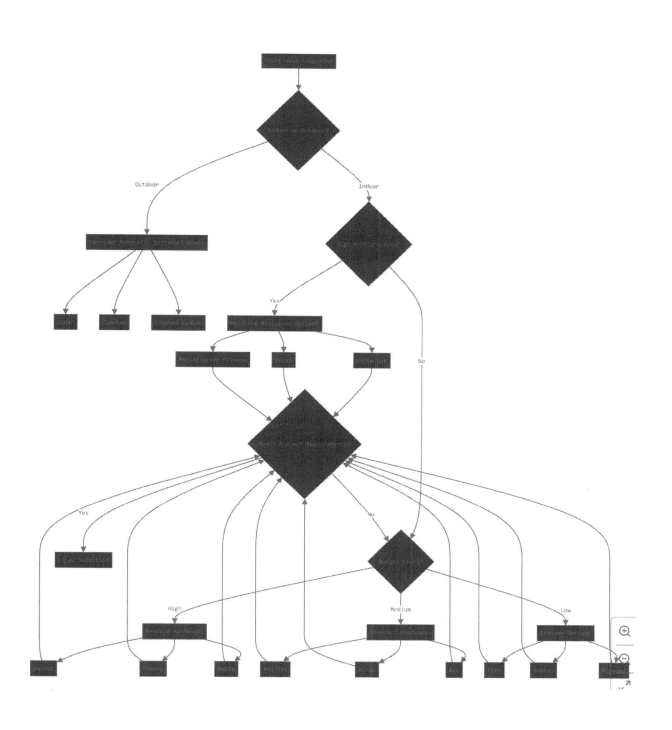

Wood Properties Guide

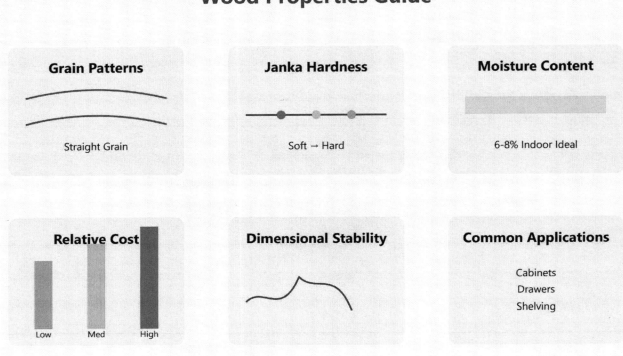

Grain Patterns

Straight Grain

Janka Hardness

Soft → Hard

Moisture Content

6-8% Indoor Ideal

Relative Cost

Low   Med   High

Dimensional Stability

Common Applications

Cabinets
Drawers
Shelving

Essential Hardware and Fasteners

Let's dive into the crucial world of hardware and fasteners -
the components that quite literally hold your storage projects
together. Understanding these elements is just as important
as knowing your woods, as the right hardware can mean the
difference between a storage solution that lasts generations
and one that fails prematurely.

Understanding Hardware Categories

Hardware for storage projects falls into several key
categories, each serving specific functions:

1. Joinery Hardware
   - Screws
   - Nails
   - Bolts
   - Dowels
   - Biscuits
   - Dominos

2. Movement Hardware
   - Drawer slides
   - Hinges
   - Lid supports
   - Casters

3. Organizational Hardware
   - Shelf pins
   - Shelf standards
   - Cabinet pulls and knobs
   - Wire organizers

4. Support Hardware
   - Brackets
   - Corner braces
   - Mounting cleats
   - Support rails

Hardware Selection Process

The process of selecting appropriate hardware involves careful consideration of multiple factors:

1. Load Requirements
   - Calculate expected weight loads
   - Factor in dynamic vs. static loads
   - Consider safety margins
   - Account for material strength

2. Environmental Conditions
   - Indoor vs. outdoor use
   - Humidity exposure
   - Temperature fluctuations

- Chemical exposure (cleaning products, etc.)

3. Aesthetic Requirements
- Visible vs. hidden hardware
- Finish matching
- Style compatibility
- Period authenticity (if relevant)

Operational Sequence for Hardware Installation

1. Pre-Installation Planning
- Review project plans and identify all hardware locations
- Verify hardware compatibility with materials
- Check clearances and tolerances
- Prepare installation templates if needed
- Gather required tools and supplies

2. Hardware Preparation
- Sort hardware by type and location
- Verify all components are present
- Pre-finish hardware if required
- Prepare mounting surfaces
- Create pilot hole guides

3. Installation Process
- Mark hardware locations precisely
- Drill pilot holes when required

- Test fit before final installation
- Install in proper sequence
- Verify proper operation
- Make necessary adjustments

4. Quality Control
  - Check all fasteners for tightness
  - Verify smooth operation
  - Test load capacity
  - Inspect for proper alignment
  - Ensure proper clearances

Fastener Selection Guide

When selecting fasteners, consider these key factors:

1. Screw Selection
  - Material thickness
  - Wood species
  - Load requirements
  - Exposure conditions
  - Head style requirements

2. Proper Sizing
  - Length: Generally 2.5-3 times material thickness
  - Diameter: Based on wood density and load
  - Head size: Appropriate for application

- Thread pitch: Coarse for softwoods, fine for hardwoods

3. Material Compatibility
- Brass screws for decorative applications
- Stainless steel for moisture resistance
- Zinc-plated for general indoor use
- Bronze for specific aesthetic requirements

Best Practices for Hardware Installation

1. Pilot Holes
- Use proper drill bit sizes
- Account for wood species
- Consider grain direction
- Maintain consistent depth

2. Fastener Installation
- Use appropriate driver bits
- Maintain proper torque
- Avoid over-tightening
- Consider thread relief when needed

3. Maintenance Considerations
- Plan for future adjustments
- Allow for wood movement
- Consider replacement access
- Document hardware specifications

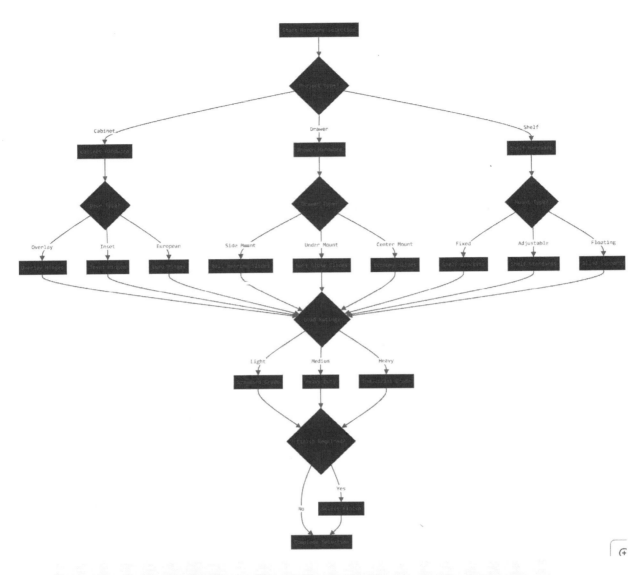

Storage Hardware Guide

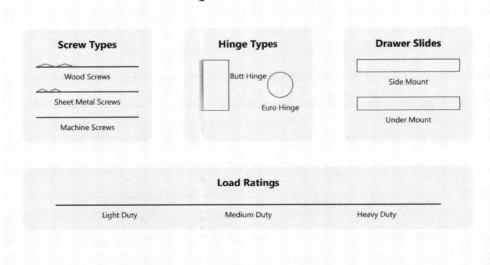

Screw Types	Hinge Types	Drawer Slides
Wood Screws	Butt Hinge	Side Mount
Sheet Metal Screws	Euro Hinge	Under Mount
Machine Screws		

Load Ratings

Light Duty   Medium Duty   Heavy Duty

Understanding Wood Movement and Seasonal Changes

Wood is a living, breathing material even after it's been cut and processed. Think of it like a bundle of straws - these cellulose fibers can absorb and release moisture, causing the wood to expand and contract throughout the year. Understanding this movement is crucial for creating storage solutions that will remain stable and functional across seasons.

The Science Behind Wood Movement

Wood movement occurs primarily due to changes in moisture content (MC). When wood absorbs moisture, its cells expand, causing the material to swell. Conversely, when wood loses moisture, the cells contract, causing shrinkage. This process happens continuously as wood responds to environmental changes in humidity and temperature.

The three primary types of wood movement are:

1. Radial Movement
   - Occurs across the growth rings
   - Generally amounts to 3-6% dimensional change
   - More stable than tangential movement

2. Tangential Movement
 - Occurs parallel to growth rings
 - Usually 6-12% dimensional change
 - Most significant type of movement

3. Longitudinal Movement
 - Occurs along the grain length
 - Minimal (typically 0.1-0.2%)
 - Generally not a significant concern in construction
```

**Managing Wood Movement in Projects**

To successfully manage wood movement in your storage projects, follow this operational sequence:

## 1. Assessment Phase
 - Measure current wood moisture content
 - Document ambient humidity levels
 - Identify seasonal humidity patterns
 - Calculate expected movement ranges

## 2. Design Considerations
 - Choose appropriate wood cuts
 - Plan for movement direction
 - Include expansion gaps
 - Select proper joinery methods
```

3. Construction Methods
- Use floating panels
- Implement slip joints
- Allow for seasonal adjustment
- Consider grain orientation

4. Implementation Steps
- Acclimate wood properly
- Monitor moisture content
- Use appropriate fasteners
- Build in adjustment allowances

Practical Solutions for Common Situations

1. Panel Construction
- Use frame-and-panel design
- Allow panels to float freely
- Size grooves appropriately
- Consider seasonal extremes

2. Drawer Construction
- Account for cross-grain movement
- Use appropriate slides
- Allow clearance for expansion
- Consider seasonal adjustments

3. Cabinet Construction
  - Design proper door clearances
  - Use appropriate hinges
  - Allow for panel movement
  - Consider seasonal adjustments

Best Practices for Movement Management

1. Material Selection
  - Choose quarter-sawn lumber for stability
  - Use properly dried wood
  - Consider engineered products
  - Match wood species to environment

2. Design Elements
  - Include expansion gaps
  - Use floating panels
  - Allow for movement
  - Plan for adjustments

3. Construction Techniques
  - Use appropriate joinery
  - Allow for wood movement
  - Include adjustment features
  - Monitor and maintain

Monitoring and Maintenance

1. Regular Inspection
   - Check moisture content
   - Monitor joint movement
   - Observe seasonal changes
   - Document changes

2. Adjustment Procedures
   - Adjust hardware as needed
   - Maintain proper gaps
   - Monitor humidity levels
   - Make seasonal adjustments

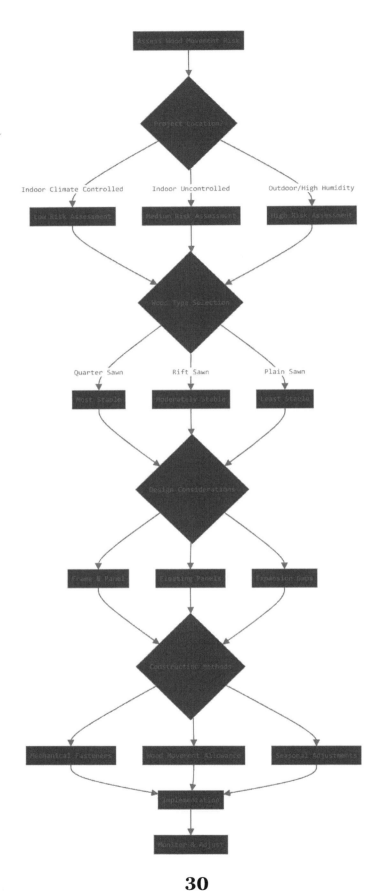

Assess Wood Movement Risk

Project Location?

Indoor Climate Controlled — Low Risk Assessment

Indoor Uncontrolled — Medium Risk Assessment

Outdoor/High Humidity — High Risk Assessment

Wood Type Selection

Quarter Sawn — Most Stable

Rift Sawn — Moderately Stable

Plain Sawn — Least Stable

Design Considerations

Frame & Panel

Floating Panels

Expansion Gaps

Construction Methods

Mechanical Fasteners

Wood Movement Allowance

Seasonal Adjustments

Implementation

Monitor & Adjust

Wood Movement Patterns

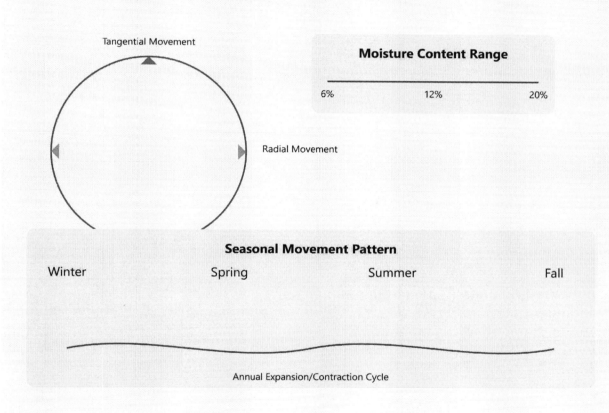

Tangential Movement

Radial Movement

Moisture Content Range

6%   12%   20%

Seasonal Movement Pattern

Winter   Spring   Summer   Fall

Annual Expansion/Contraction Cycle

Tools Required for Storage Projects

Let me guide you through the essential tools needed for creating storage solutions, starting from basic hand tools to more specialized power equipment. We'll explore not just what tools you need, but how to select, use, and maintain them properly.

Understanding Tool Categories

Tools for storage projects can be organized into four main categories:

1. Measuring and Layout Tools
   - Essential for accurate planning and execution
   - Forms the foundation of all woodworking
   - Critical for project success
   - Requires regular calibration and care

2. Cutting Tools
   - Both hand and power options
   - Varies by project complexity
   - Determines quality of joints
   - Impacts overall finish

3. Assembly Tools
   - Critical for joining components

- Affects structural integrity
- Determines work efficiency
- Influences final quality

4. Finishing Tools
- Impacts final appearance
- Affects durability
- Determines surface quality
- Essential for protection

Essential Tool List and Their Uses

1. Measuring and Layout Tools
- Tape Measure (25' minimum)
- Combination Square
- Marking Gauge
- Level (2' and 4')
- Marking Knife
- Pencils and Marking Tools

2. Cutting Tools
- Circular Saw
- Table Saw
- Jigsaw
- Hand Saws
- Chisels
- Router

3. Assembly Tools
 - Drill/Driver
 - Clamps (various sizes)
 - Hammer
 - Screwdrivers
 - Mallets
 - Assembly Square

4. Finishing Tools
 - Random Orbital Sander
 - Hand Sanders
 - Brushes
 - Spray Equipment
 - Finishing Supplies

Tool Selection Process

1. Project Assessment
 - Evaluate project complexity
 - Determine required precision
 - Consider material types
 - Assess budget constraints

2. Tool Evaluation
 - Research tool options
 - Compare features
 - Read reviews
 - Consider future needs

3. Purchase Planning
   - Prioritize essential tools
   - Plan for upgrades
   - Consider quality vs. cost
   - Research warranties

Tool Setup and Maintenance

1. Initial Setup
   - Unpack and inspect
   - Calibrate and adjust
   - Test operation
   - Document settings

2. Regular Maintenance
   - Clean after use
   - Check calibration
   - Lubricate moving parts
   - Inspect for wear

3. Storage and Organization
   - Create dedicated spaces
   - Protect from moisture
   - Maintain accessibility
   - Label and organize

Safety Equipment

1. Personal Protection
- Safety glasses
- Hearing protection
- Dust mask/respirator
- Work gloves

2. Workshop Safety
- First aid kit
- Fire extinguisher
- Dust collection
- Adequate lighting

Tool Usage Best Practices

1. Before Use
- Check condition
- Verify settings
- Clear workspace
- Review safety procedures

2. During Use
- Maintain proper stance
- Use appropriate pressure
- Monitor tool performance
- Watch for issues

3. After Use
   - Clean thoroughly
   - Inspect for damage
   - Store properly
   - Document maintenance

Tool Investment Strategy

1. Essential First Purchases
   - Quality measuring tools
   - Basic power tools
   - Essential hand tools
   - Safety equipment

2. Intermediate Additions
   - Specialized cutting tools
   - Advanced measuring tools
   - Additional clamps
   - Power sanders

3. Advanced Equipment
   - Professional-grade tools
   - Specialized jigs
   - Advanced power tools
   - Precision instruments

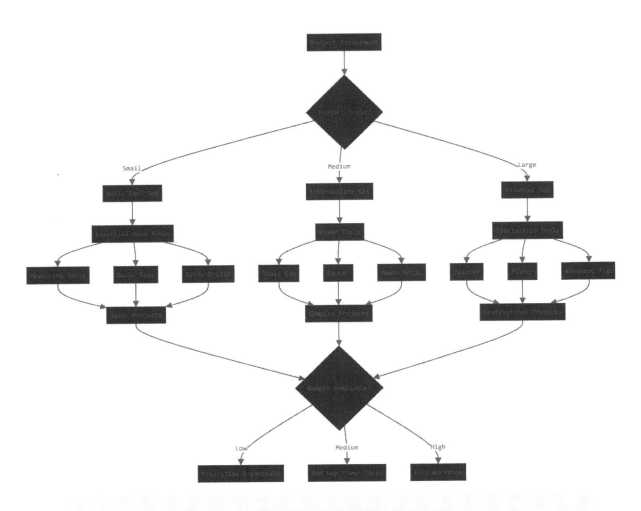

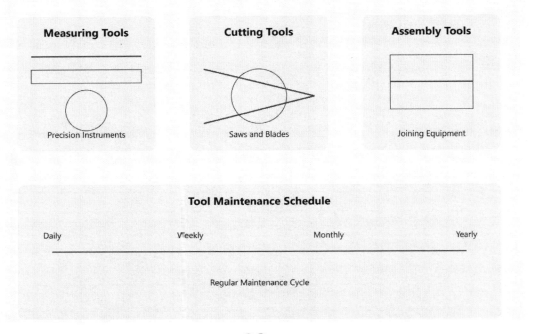

Workshop Tool Organization

Measuring Tools

Precision Instruments

Cutting Tools

Saws and Blades

Assembly Tools

Joining Equipment

Tool Maintenance Schedule

Daily   Weekly   Monthly   Yearly

Regular Maintenance Cycle

Chapter 2
Project Planning and Design

Reading and Creating Project Plans

Let me guide you through the essential process of reading and creating project plans for storage solutions. Think of project plans as the roadmap for your woodworking journey - they're not just drawings, but a comprehensive communication tool that guides every step of your build.

Understanding Project Plans

Project plans consist of several key components that work together to provide a complete picture of the project:

1. Orthographic Projections
   - Front elevation (front view)
   - Side elevation (side view)
   - Top view (plan view)
   - Interior details
   - Section views

2. Detailed Drawings
   - Joinery details
   - Hardware placement

- Assembly sequences
- Critical dimensions

3. Supporting Documentation
   - Materials list
   - Cut list
   - Hardware schedule
   - Construction notes

Creating Project Plans: Step-by-Step Process

1. Initial Planning Phase
   a. Gather Requirements
   - Interview client or define personal needs
   - Document specific requirements
   - Establish budget constraints
   - Define timeline expectations

   b. Space Assessment
   - Measure available space
   - Note any obstacles or constraints
   - Consider access requirements
   - Document existing conditions

2. Conceptual Design Phase
   a. Preliminary Sketches
   - Create rough sketches
   - Explore multiple options **40**

- Consider proportions
- Test different layouts

b. Design Development
- Refine basic dimensions
- Determine material requirements
- Consider construction methods
- Plan hardware placement

3. Detailed Design Phase
a. Create Working Drawings
- Draw to scale
- Include all dimensions
- Show construction details
- Indicate materials

b. Develop Supporting Documentation
- Create cut lists
- Compile materials list
- Document hardware requirements
- Write construction notes

Reading Project Plans

1. Understanding Symbols and Conventions
- Learn standard symbols
- Understand line types

41

- Recognize dimension standards
- Interpret notes and callouts

2. Analyzing Views
- Study relationships between views
- Understand hidden lines
- Interpret section views
- Review detail callouts

3. Working with Dimensions
- Verify overall dimensions
- Check individual components
- Understand tolerances
- Calculate material requirements

Plan Review and Verification

1. Quality Control Checks
- Verify dimensions
- Check scale accuracy
- Review material specifications
- Confirm hardware details

2. Constructability Review
- Assess building sequence
- Verify tool requirements
- Check material availability

- Consider workshop limitations

3. Documentation Review
 - Verify completeness
 - Check for conflicts
 - Review notes and specifications
 - Confirm material lists

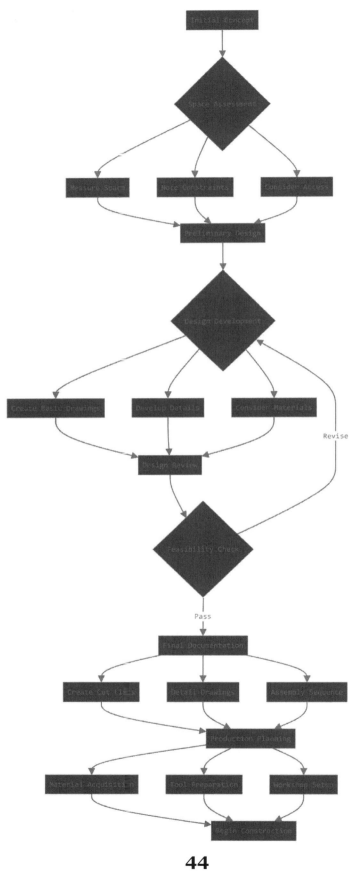

Project Plan Components

Orthographic Views

Front   Side

Detail Views

Joinery   Hardware

Dimensions

Critical Measurements

Supporting Documentation

Cut List

Materials List

Construction Notes

Measuring and Marking Techniques

Let me guide you through the critical art of measuring and marking, which forms the foundation of all successful woodworking projects. Think of measuring and marking as creating a precise roadmap on your materials – every line you draw and measurement you make will directly influence the quality of your final piece.

Understanding Precision and Accuracy

When we talk about measuring and marking in woodworking, we need to understand the difference between precision and accuracy. Precision refers to the consistency of measurements, while accuracy relates to how close these measurements are to the true value. In woodworking, we often need both, but sometimes precision is more important than absolute accuracy, especially when working with relative measurements.

Essential Tools and Their Proper Usage

Let's explore the key tools and how to use them effectively:

1. Measuring Tools
   - Tape measure: Always hook the end properly, accounting for the sliding mechanism

- Steel rule: Use the graduated edge directly against the work surface
- Digital calipers: Zero before each use, keep measuring surfaces clean
- Combination square: Check squareness regularly, maintain tight adjustments
- Marking gauge: Set once and lock firmly for consistent marks

2. Marking Tools

- Marking knife: Hold at a consistent angle, use light pressure
- Pencils: Keep sharp, use appropriate hardness (4H for fine lines, 2B for rough marking)
- Marking awl: Apply consistent pressure, maintain sharp point
- Carpenter's square: Check for accuracy periodically
- Sliding bevel: Lock securely after setting angles

Measuring and Marking Process

Let's break down the process into clear, sequential steps:

1. Initial Setup

- Clean and prepare work surface
- Gather all necessary tools
- Ensure proper lighting
- Verify tool accuracy

- Set reference edges

2. Taking Measurements
- Choose appropriate measuring tool
- Account for tool characteristics
- Consider material thickness
- Allow for cutting allowance
- Document measurements

3. Marking Process
- Establish reference lines
- Use appropriate marking tool
- Create clear, visible marks
- Double-check measurements
- Mark cutting lines

4. Verification
- Recheck all measurements
- Verify square and parallel
- Confirm allowances
- Document final dimensions
- Test fit when possible

Common Measuring and Marking Errors to Avoid

Understanding typical errors helps prevent them:

1. Measurement Errors
   - Parallax error from incorrect viewing angle
   - Tape measure hook compensation
   - Accumulated error in sequential measurements
   - Temperature effects on metal rules

2. Marking Errors
   - Inconsistent marking pressure
   - Dull marking tools
   - Inadequate lighting
   - Unstable workpiece

Best Practices for Accuracy

1. Reference Surfaces
   - Establish clear reference edges
   - Mark reference faces
   - Maintain consistent orientation
   - Use stable work support

2. Tool Maintenance
   - Regular calibration checks
   - Clean measuring surfaces
   - Sharp marking tools

- Proper tool storage

3. Working Methods
- Use consistent pressure
- Mark from reference edges
- Double-check measurements
- Document critical dimensions

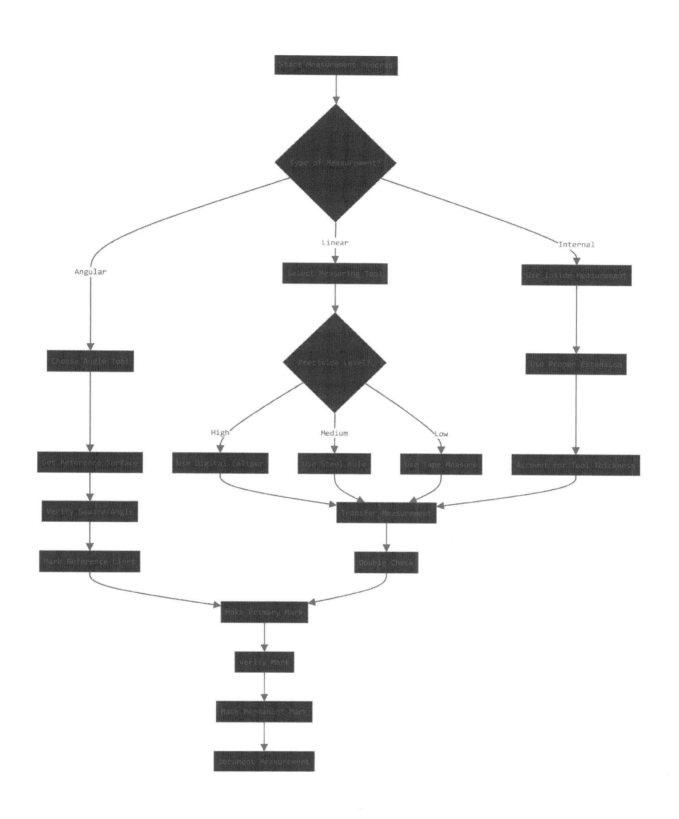

Measuring and Marking Guide

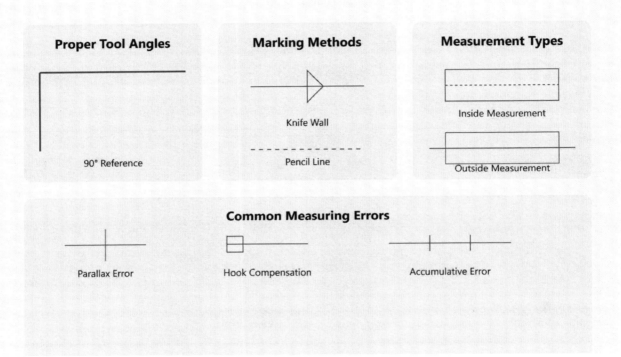

Proper Tool Angles

90° Reference

Marking Methods

Knife Wall

Pencil Line

Measurement Types

Inside Measurement

Outside Measurement

Common Measuring Errors

Parallax Error

Hook Compensation

Accumulative Error

Calculating Material Requirements

Think of this as creating a detailed shopping list that ensures you'll have exactly what you need when you need it, while minimizing waste and controlling costs. This skill forms the foundation of efficient project management in woodworking.

Understanding Material Calculations

Material calculations involve more than just adding up the dimensions of your finished pieces. We need to account for several factors that influence the total amount of material needed:

1. Dimensional Considerations

When we calculate materials, we must consider three key dimensions:
- Rough dimensions (the size of raw material)
- Working dimensions (size after initial milling)
- Final dimensions (size of finished pieces)

2. Waste Factors

We need to account for several types of waste:
- Saw kerf (typically 1/8" for standard blades)
- Planing allowance (usually 1/4" total thickness)
- Jointing allowance (approximately 1/8" per edge)
- Defect allowance (varies by material grade)

- Safety margin (typically 10-15% extra)

Material Calculation Process

Let's break down the calculation process into manageable steps:

1. Project Analysis Phase
   In this initial phase, we examine our project plans to understand exactly what we need:
   - Study project drawings thoroughly
   - List all components by size
   - Note grain direction requirements
   - Identify material specifications
   - Consider construction sequence

2. Component Calculation
   For each component, calculate:
   - Final dimensions required
   - Working dimensions needed
   - Rough dimensions to start with
   - Grain matching requirements
   - Quantity needed including spares

3. Material Optimization
   Create a cutting diagram to:
   - Minimize waste
   - Match grain patterns

- Account for defects
- Optimize sheet usage
- Plan cutting sequence

4. Waste Factor Calculation
 Add appropriate allowances for:
 - Saw kerrf (blade thickness)
 - Planing allowance
 - Jointing allowance
 - End trimming
 - Defect removal

Practical Calculation Examples

Let's look at some real-world calculations:

For Sheet Goods:
1. Calculate net area needed:
 - Sum all component areas
 - Add 10% for waste
 - Account for grain direction
 - Consider standard sheet sizes

For Dimensional Lumber:

1. Calculate board feet:
   - Thickness $\times$ Width $\times$ Length $\div$ 144
   - Add 15% for waste
   - Account for rough dimensioning
   - Consider standard lengths

Material List Creation

Develop a comprehensive material list including:

1. Primary Materials
   - Sheet goods specifications
   - Lumber requirements
   - Hardware components
   - Finishing materials

2. Supporting Materials
   - Adhesives
   - Fasteners
   - Shop supplies
   - Finishing supplies

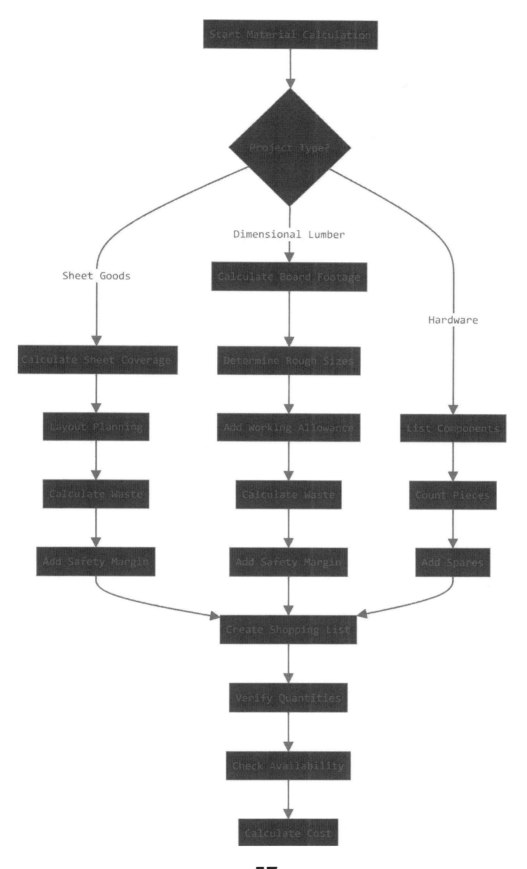

Material Calculation Guide

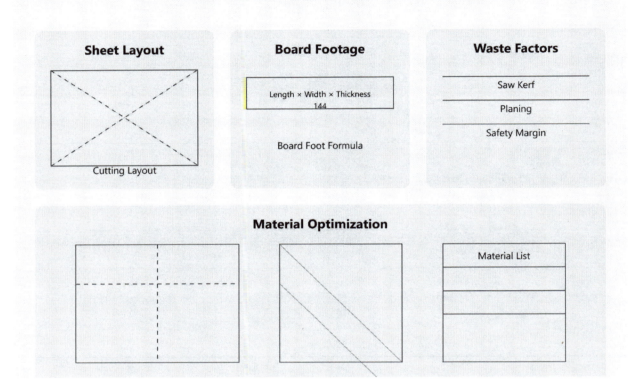

Sheet Layout

Cutting Layout

Board Footage

Length × Width × Thickness
144

Board Foot Formula

Waste Factors

Saw Kerf

Planing

Safety Margin

Material Optimization

Material List

Design Considerations for Different Spaces

Let me guide you through the intricate process of designing storage solutions for various spaces. Think of each space as having its own personality and needs - just as we adapt our behavior to different environments, our storage solutions must adapt to different spaces while maintaining functionality and aesthetic harmony.

Understanding Space Analysis

When we approach a new space for storage design, we need to consider multiple layers of analysis:

1. Physical Constraints

The actual dimensions are just the beginning. We need to understand:
   - Ceiling height and any variations
   - Floor levelness and load capacity
   - Wall construction and support capability
   - Door swing arcs and clearances
   - Window locations and natural light patterns
   - Electrical outlet and switch locations
   - HVAC register positions and airflow patterns

2. Environmental Factors

The space's environment significantly impacts design choices:
- Temperature fluctuations
- Humidity levels and variations
- Natural and artificial lighting
- Air circulation patterns
- Exposure to direct sunlight
- Potential water exposure
- Dust and debris levels### Design Process for Different Spaces

Let's walk through the systematic approach to designing storage for various spaces:

1. Initial Space Assessment

First, we conduct a thorough analysis of the space:
- Measure all dimensions precisely
- Document existing features and obstacles
- Note traffic patterns and flow
- Identify lighting conditions
- Record environmental factors
- Consider user accessibility needs

2. Function Analysis

Understanding how the space will be used:
- Identify primary activities

- List storage requirements
- Consider frequency of access
- Note size ranges of items
- Plan for future expansion
- Account for seasonal variations

3. Design Development
Creating solutions that match the space:
- Sketch preliminary layouts
- Consider modular options
- Plan vertical space usage
- Design appropriate depths
- Include proper clearances
- Account for ventilation needs

4. Material Selection
Choosing appropriate materials based on:
- Environmental conditions
- Usage patterns
- Load requirements
- Aesthetic preferences
- Budget constraints
- Maintenance needs

Space-Specific Considerations

Let's examine specific considerations for different types of spaces:

1. Kitchen Storage
   - Consider heat exposure near appliances
   - Plan for moisture resistance
   - Include ventilation for food storage
   - Design for easy cleaning
   - Account for heavy items
   - Plan workflow efficiency

2. Workshop Storage
   - Design for tool accessibility
   - Include dust protection
   - Plan for power tool storage
   - Consider safety requirements
   - Include workspace clearance
   - Account for material storage

3. Closet Storage
   - Maximize vertical space
   - Include various hanging heights
   - Plan for seasonal rotation
   - Design for easy access
   - Include proper ventilation
   - Consider lighting needs

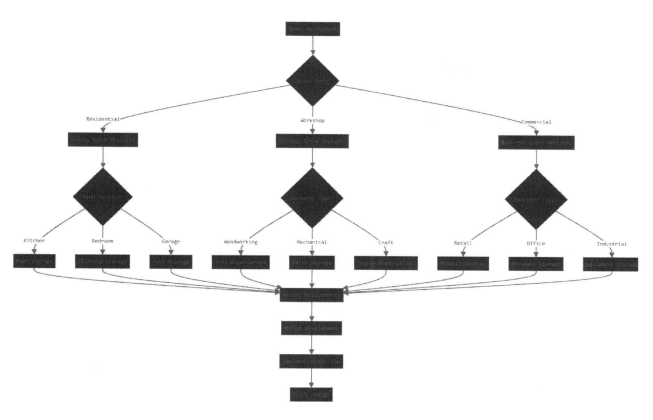

Space Design Elements

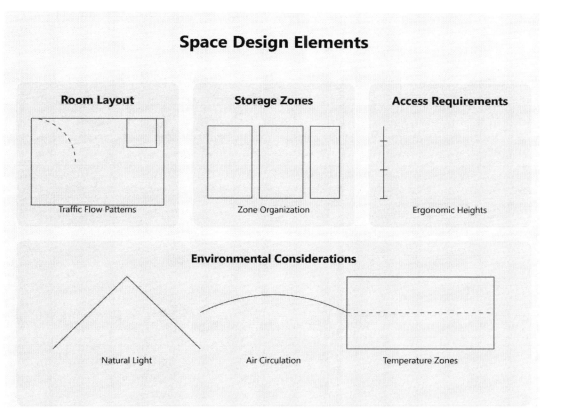

Room Layout	Storage Zones	Access Requirements
Traffic Flow Patterns	Zone Organization	Ergonomic Heights

Environmental Considerations

Natural Light　　　Air Circulation　　　Temperature Zones

PART II
FUNDAMENTAL
TECHNIQUES

Chapter 3
Basic Box Construction

Understanding Box Joints and Joinery Methods

Let me guide you through the fascinating world of box joinery. Think of box joints as the interlocking pieces of a puzzle - when crafted correctly, they create connections that are both beautiful and incredibly strong. Just as a chain is only as strong as its weakest link, a box is only as sturdy as its joints.

Understanding Box Joint Fundamentals

Box joints consist of interlocking fingers that create a strong mechanical connection between two pieces of wood. The strength comes from three key factors:

First, the increased gluing surface area created by the fingers provides more bonding strength than a simple butt joint.

Second, the interlocking nature of the joints creates mechanical resistance to pulling forces. Third, the grain orientation of the fingers prevents wood movement from weakening the joint over time.

Step-by-Step Box Joint Creation Process

Let me walk you through the process of creating perfect box joints:

1. Material Preparation
 Begin with stock that's precisely milled to uniform thickness and width:
 - Surface all faces until they're perfectly flat
 - Joint one edge perfectly square
 - Rip to final width ensuring parallel edges
 - Cut pieces to final length with square ends

2. Layout and Marking
 Careful layout is crucial for successful joints:
 - Mark reference faces and edges
 - Determine finger width based on material thickness
 - Layout joint pattern on both mating pieces
 - Double-check all measurements
 - Mark waste areas clearly

3. Creating the Joints
The cutting process requires patience and precision:
- Set up appropriate jig (table saw or router)
- Make test cuts on scrap material
- Adjust settings for perfect fit
- Cut all fingers, working from layout lines
- Keep consistent pressure against fence
- Make multiple light passes if needed

4. Test Fitting
Proper test fitting helps ensure success:
- Dry fit joints before applying glue
- Check for square corners
- Verify full finger engagement
- Look for any gaps or tight spots
- Make adjustments as needed

Common Box Joint Variations

Let's explore different types of box joints:

1. Through Box Joints
The most common variation:
- Fingers visible on both faces
- Equal finger spacing
- Full material thickness
- Maximum gluing surface

2. Half-Blind Box Joints
Used when one side should be hidden:
- Fingers visible on one face only
- Requires more precise cutting
- Often used in drawer construction
- Provides clean appearance

3. Stopped Box Joints
A decorative variation:
- Fingers don't extend full width
- Creates unique appearance
- More challenging to execute
- Requires careful planning

Key Considerations for Success

To create strong, attractive box joints, keep these factors in mind:

1. Material Selection
Choose appropriate stock:
- Straight-grained wood
- Stable species
- Consistent density
- Free of defects

2. Tool Selection
Use the right tools:
- Sharp cutting tools
- Appropriate jigs
- Accurate measuring tools
- Proper clamps

3. Environmental Factors
Consider working conditions:
- Stable temperature
- Controlled humidity
- Good lighting
- Clean work surface

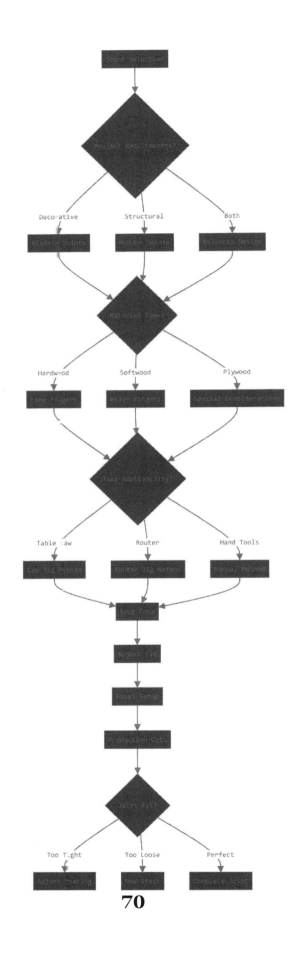

Box Joint Anatomy

Basic Joint Types

Through Joint

Half Blind Joint

Finger Spacing

Equal Spacing

Grain Orientation

Grain Direction Impact

Assembly Sequence

Cut Fingers

Test Fit

Apply Glue

Clamp Assembly

Building Strong Corners

Let me guide you through the essential process of building strong corners, which form the backbone of any storage project. Think of corners as the shoulders of your project - they bear significant weight and stress while maintaining the structure's integrity. Just as a house needs a solid foundation, a storage piece needs robust corners to stand the test of time.

Understanding Corner Strength Principles

When we talk about corner strength, we're really discussing three fundamental forces that corners must resist:

The first is racking force - the diagonal pressure that tries to collapse your box into a parallelogram. Imagine pushing the top of a box sideways while holding the bottom still - that's racking force.

The second is pulling force - the outward pressure that attempts to separate the corner joints. This commonly occurs when drawers or doors are opened repeatedly.

The third is compression force - the downward pressure that pushes the corners together, typically from weight placed on or in the storage piece.

Building Strong Corners: Step-by-Step Process

Let me walk you through the systematic approach to creating robust corners:

1. Material Selection and Preparation
First, we need to ensure our materials are properly prepared:
 - Select straight-grained wood for maximum strength
 - Mill all pieces to exact thickness and width
 - Ensure ends are perfectly square
 - Check moisture content is appropriate
 - Identify and mark reference faces

2. Joint Selection and Preparation
Based on your project requirements, choose an appropriate joint:
 - Consider load requirements
 - Account for visual preferences
 - Factor in available tools
 - Think about assembly sequence
 - Plan for any reinforcement

3. Cutting and Fitting Process
Execute the joint with careful attention to detail:
 - Make test cuts on scrap material
 - Verify all settings and measurements
 - Cut joints slightly tight
 - Test fit without glue

- Make any necessary adjustments

4. Assembly and Reinforcement
Proper assembly ensures joint strength:
- Clean all mating surfaces
- Apply glue appropriately
- Use proper clamping pressure
- Add reinforcement if needed
- Check for square during assembly

Corner Joint Types and Their Applications

Let's explore different corner joint options:

1. Basic Butt Joint with Reinforcement
Perfect for simple projects:
- Easy to cut and assemble
- Requires reinforcement
- Good for painted pieces
- Economical solution
- Quick to produce

2. Miter Joint Variations
Creates clean, professional corners:
- Hides end grain
- Can be reinforced with splines
- Requires precise cutting

- Good for decorative pieces
- Multiple reinforcement options

3. Advanced Mechanical Joints

Maximum strength without reinforcement:
- Box joints for maximum glue surface
- Dovetails for traditional strength
- Lock miters for clean looks
- Finger joints for modern appeal
- Specialized joints for specific needs

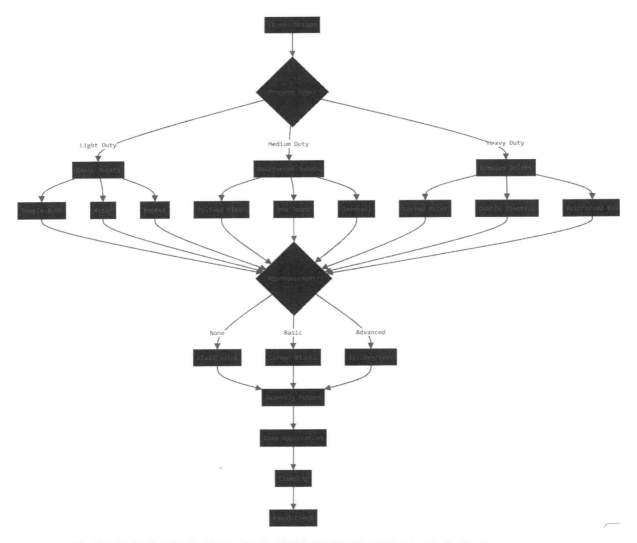

Corner Construction Guide

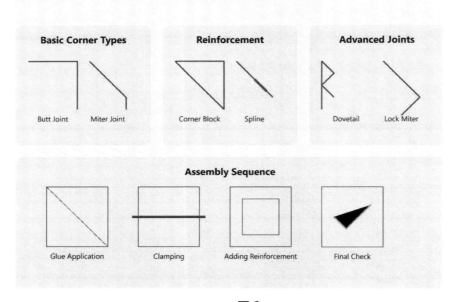

Basic Corner Types

Butt Joint   Miter Joint

Reinforcement

Corner Block   Spline

Advanced Joints

Dovetail   Lock Miter

Assembly Sequence

Glue Application   Clamping   Adding Reinforcement   Final Check

Bottom and Back Panel Installation

Let me guide you through the crucial process of installing bottom and back panels in storage projects. Think of these panels as the foundation and spine of your piece - while they might seem simple, their proper installation is vital for both structural integrity and long-term stability. Just as a house needs a solid foundation and strong walls, your storage piece needs well-fitted bottom and back panels to maintain its shape and strength.

Understanding Panel Functions and Requirements

Bottom and back panels serve multiple critical functions in storage pieces:

The bottom panel provides structural support and prevents racking (diagonal movement), while distributing weight evenly across the base. Think of it like the foundation of a house - it needs to be strong enough to support the contents while maintaining the box's shape.

The back panel maintains squareness and prevents racking in the vertical plane. It acts like a building's shear wall, providing crucial diagonal bracing that keeps corners square and stable. Additionally, it encloses the space and can contribute significantly to the piece's overall appearance.

77

Panel Installation Process: Step-by-Step Guide

Let's walk through the systematic process of installing both bottom and back panels:

1. Planning and Preparation
First, we need to carefully plan our approach:
- Measure case dimensions precisely
- Account for wood movement
- Choose appropriate material
- Determine mounting method
- Plan for any reinforcement

2. Bottom Panel Installation
The process varies by mounting method:

For Dado Mount:
- Cut dado grooves in side pieces
- Size panel allowing for movement
- Test fit panel in grooves
- Apply glue if needed
- Insert panel during assembly

For Rabbet Mount:
- Cut rabbets in side pieces
- Size panel precisely
- Add support cleats if needed

- Install panel during assembly
- Secure with screws or nails

3. Back Panel Installation
Several methods are available:

For Rabbet Mount:
- Cut rabbet in case back
- Size panel with expansion gap
- Test fit panel in rabbet
- Secure with appropriate fasteners
- Add cleats if needed

For Dado Mount:
- Cut dados in all sides
- Size panel precisely
- Test fit thoroughly
- Install during assembly
- Allow for movement

4. Panel Material Selection
Choose appropriate materials based on needs:

For Bottom Panels:
- Solid wood for traditional pieces
- Plywood for stability
- MDF for painted pieces

- Hardboard for light duty
- Consider thickness requirements

For Back Panels:
- 1/4" plywood common choice
- Solid wood for high-end pieces
- Hardboard for economy
- Consider visibility
- Match grain if exposed

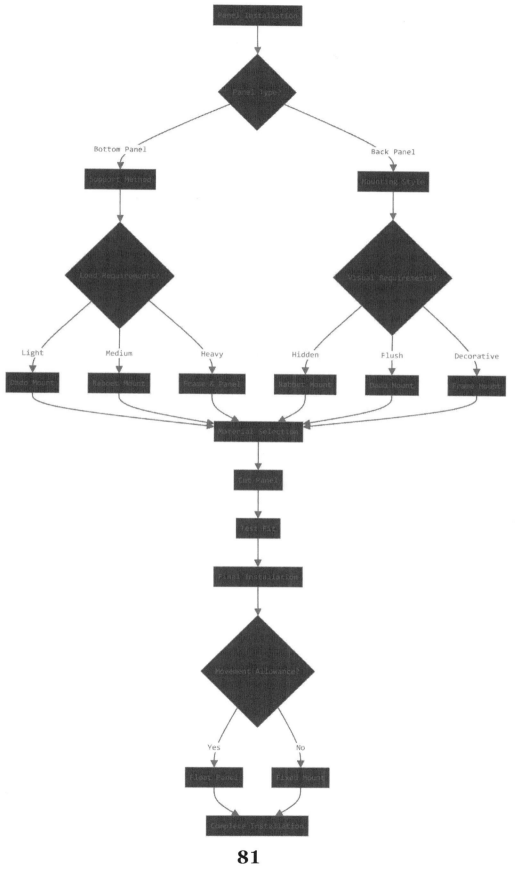

81

Panel Installation Methods

Bottom Panel Mounting

Dado Mount

Back Panel Options

Rabbet Mount

Movement Allowance

Expansion Space

Installation Process

Panel Sizing

Groove Details

Final Assembly

Adding Dividers and Compartments

Let me guide you through the process of adding dividers and compartments to your storage projects. Think of dividers as the interior walls of your piece - just as rooms in a house serve different purposes and organize space efficiently, dividers and compartments transform a simple box into a highly functional storage solution.

Understanding Divider Types and Functions

Interior organization begins with understanding three primary types of dividers:

Fixed dividers provide permanent structure and often contribute to the overall strength of the piece. Like load-bearing walls in a building, they can help distribute weight and prevent racking while creating distinct storage areas.

Adjustable dividers offer flexibility, allowing the space to be reconfigured as needs change. These are similar to moveable shelving systems, providing versatility without sacrificing stability.

Removable dividers create temporary compartments that can be completely removed when needed. These are particularly useful for items that vary in size or when maximum space is occasionally needed.

Step-by-Step Divider Installation Process

Let me walk you through the comprehensive process of adding dividers and compartments:

1. Planning Phase
Begin with careful planning to ensure success:
  - Measure interior space precisely
  - Determine desired compartment sizes
  - Consider item sizes to be stored
  - Plan for material thickness
  - Account for hardware clearance

2. Material Selection
Choose appropriate materials based on needs:
  - Match or complement case materials
  - Consider load requirements
  - Account for movement potential
  - Select appropriate thickness
  - Consider visibility of edges

3. Layout and Marking
Accurate layout is crucial:
  - Mark centerlines clearly
  - Account for material thickness
  - Mark all dado locations
  - Double-check measurements
  - Consider grain direction   **84**

4. Cutting Joinery
Different mounting methods require specific approaches:

For Fixed Dividers:
- Cut dados in case sides
- Size dividers precisely
- Test fit thoroughly
- Prepare for assembly
- Plan glue strategy

For Adjustable Systems:
- Install track hardware
- Cut slots if needed
- Prepare mounting clips
- Test adjustment range
- Verify smooth operation

5. Installation Process
Follow a logical sequence:

For Permanent Installation:
- Dry fit all components
- Apply glue if needed
- Install in correct order
- Check for square
- Allow glue to cure

For Adjustable Systems:
- Mount tracks securely
- Install support hardware
- Test operation
- Make adjustments
- Verify stability

Tips for Successful Divider Installation

1. Layout Considerations
- Start with larger divisions
- Work systematically
- Consider future flexibility
- Plan for odd sizes
- Leave adjustment room

2. Installation Techniques
- Use consistent pressure
- Keep edges clean
- Check for square
- Test fit frequently
- Work methodically

3. Quality Control
- Verify measurements
- Check all joints
- Test movement
- Ensure stability
- Clean thoroughly

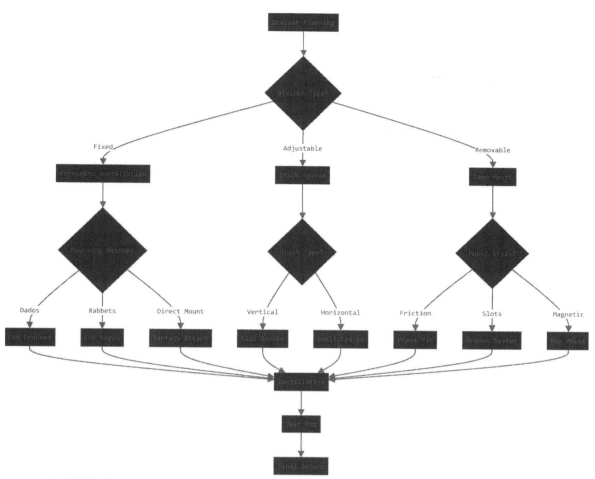

Divider Installation Methods

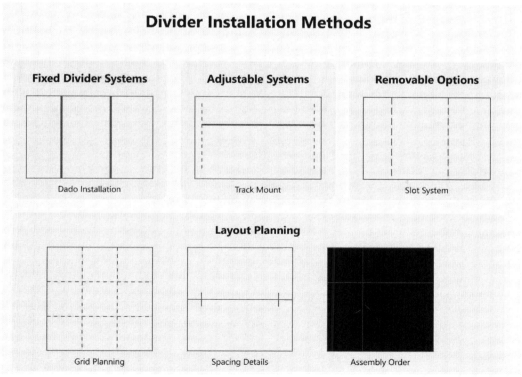

Fixed Divider Systems

Dado Installation

Adjustable Systems

Track Mount

Removable Options

Slot System

Layout Planning

Grid Planning

Spacing Details

Assembly Order

Chapter 4
Cabinet Construction Fundamentals

Cabinet Box Assembly

Let me guide you through the fundamental process of cabinet box assembly. Think of a cabinet box as the skeleton of your project - just like a building needs a strong frame before adding walls and finishes, your cabinet needs a precisely assembled box to support all other components. The success of your entire project hinges on getting this foundation right.

Understanding Cabinet Box Construction

A cabinet box consists of several key components working together to create a strong, square structure:

The sides provide vertical support and mounting surfaces for hardware. Like the columns of a building, they must be perfectly plumb and parallel to ensure proper door and drawer operation.

The top and bottom rails or panels create the horizontal framework. These elements, similar to floor joists in construction, maintain the cabinet's shape and provide mounting points for shelves and other components.

Face frames (in traditional cabinets) or edge banding (in frameless cabinets) provide rigidity and a finished appearance. Think of these as the trim work that both strengthens and beautifies the structure.

Cabinet Box Assembly Process

Let me walk you through the systematic process of assembling a cabinet box:

1. Component Preparation
Begin with thorough preparation:
 - Mill all pieces to final dimensions
 - Mark reference faces and edges
 - Label all components clearly
 - Organize pieces by function
 - Verify all measurements

2. Joinery Preparation
Different cabinet styles require specific approaches:

For Face Frame Cabinets:
 - Cut dados for bottoms and tops
 - Prepare rabbet joints for backs
 - Cut face frame joints
 - Size face frame pieces
 - Pre-finish as needed

For Frameless Cabinets:
- Prepare edge banding
- Cut panel dados
- Drill shelf pin holes
- Prepare hardware locations
- Plan assembly sequence

3. Assembly Sequence
Follow a logical order:

First Stage:
- Begin with base assembly
- Install bottom panel
- Attach sides sequentially
- Check for square
- Secure temporary bracing

Second Stage:
- Install top panel or rails
- Add internal supports
- Check diagonal measurements
- Verify all joints are tight
- Install back panel

Final Stage:
- Add face frame if needed
- Install shelf supports
- Apply edge treatments   **91**

- Check all dimensions
- Verify operation

4. Quality Control Steps
Maintain accuracy throughout:
  - Check squareness frequently
  - Verify all dimensions
  - Test component fit
  - Examine joint quality
  - Confirm proper alignment

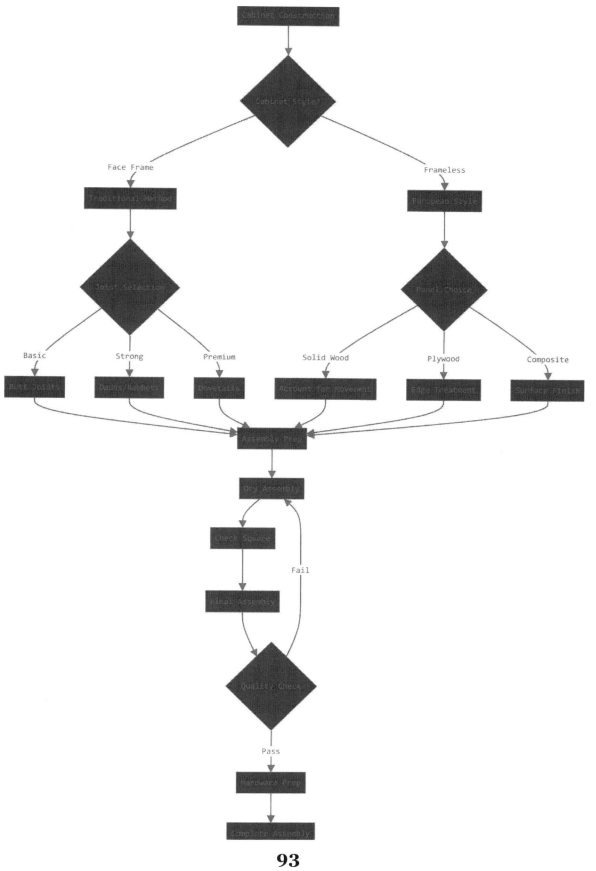

Cabinet Construction Guide

Face Frame Cabinet

Traditional Construction

Frameless Cabinet

European Style

Joint Options

Common Joints

Assembly Sequence

Component Layout

Assembly Check

Final Square Check

Installing Cabinet Backs

Let me guide you through the crucial process of installing cabinet backs. Think of a cabinet back as more than just a closure panel - it's like the spine of your cabinet, providing essential structural support and preventing racking (twisting) of the entire piece. Just as a building needs proper bracing to stay square and stable, your cabinet needs a correctly installed back panel to maintain its shape and strength throughout years of use.

Understanding Back Panel Functions

The back panel serves three critical functions in cabinet construction:

First, it provides structural rigidity by preventing the cabinet from racking or twisting. When properly installed, the back panel acts like diagonal bracing, keeping the cabinet square and stable.

Second, it creates a finished appearance and protects the contents from dust and debris. Think of it as the wall that completes your cabinet's enclosure while adding a professional finish.

Third, it can serve as a mounting surface for the cabinet itself, allowing secure attachment to walls when needed. This is particularly important for wall-mounted cabinets where the back panel must transfer the cabinet's weight to the wall structure.

Step-by-Step Back Panel Installation Process

Let me walk you through the systematic process of installing a cabinet back:

1. Preparation Phase
Begin with careful planning and preparation:
 - Measure cabinet opening precisely
 - Consider panel material options
 - Account for movement in solid wood
 - Plan mounting method
 - Gather necessary tools and fasteners

2. Panel Sizing
Accurate sizing is crucial for proper fit:
 - Measure cabinet dimensions
 - Account for rabbets or dados
 - Include expansion space if needed
 - Cut panel slightly oversized
 - Test fit and trim to final size

3. Installation Methods

Choose the appropriate installation technique:

For Rabbet Mount:
- Clean rabbet thoroughly
- Test fit panel
- Apply adhesive if using
- Position panel carefully
- Secure with appropriate fasteners

For Surface Mount:
- Square cabinet carefully
- Position panel precisely
- Use temporary bracing
- Install fasteners systematically
- Check square after installation

For Dado Mount:
- Clean dado channels
- Test panel fit
- Apply adhesive if needed
- Slide panel into position
- Secure as required

4. Fastening Techniques
Different materials require specific approaches:

For Plywood Backs:
- Use appropriate screws
- Pre-drill when needed
- Space fasteners evenly
- Consider washer use
- Avoid over-tightening

For Solid Wood Backs:
- Allow for wood movement
- Use elongated holes
- Apply flexible mounting
- Space fasteners properly
- Monitor seasonal changes

5. Quality Control
Ensure proper installation:
- Check for square
- Verify all fasteners
- Test panel security
- Examine edges
- Clean up any squeeze-out

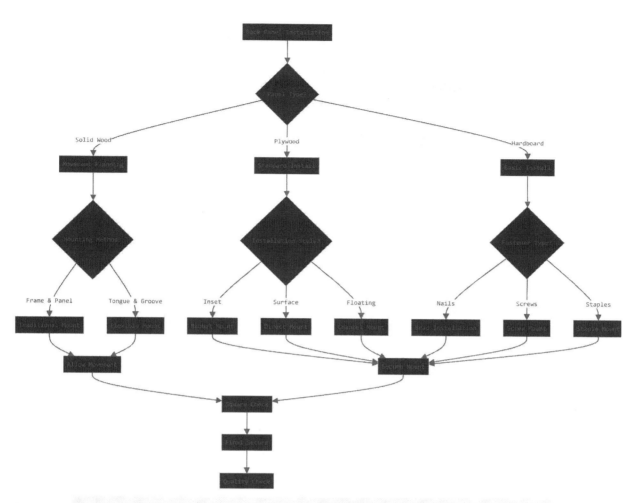

Back Panel Installation Guide

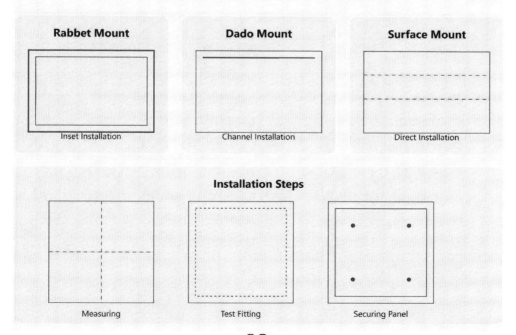

Adding Shelving and Supports

Let me guide you through the comprehensive process of adding shelves and supports to your cabinet projects. Think of shelving as the internal architecture of your cabinet - just as floors in a building need to be properly supported to carry weight safely, shelves need careful planning and installation to function reliably over time.

Understanding Shelf Support Systems

Before diving into installation, it's essential to understand how different shelf support systems work together to create safe and functional storage. Like a building's structural system, each component plays a vital role:

Fixed shelves act like the permanent floors in a building, providing maximum strength and helping to maintain the cabinet's overall rigidity. They're ideal for heavy loads and when shelf positions won't need to change.

Adjustable shelves offer flexibility similar to modular office furniture - they can be reconfigured as needs change. While typically not as strong as fixed shelves, they provide versatility that many storage situations require.

Comprehensive Installation Process

Let me walk you through the systematic process of adding shelves and supports:

1. Planning Phase
Begin with thorough planning:
 - Assess storage needs and weight requirements
 - Determine optimal shelf spacing
 - Choose appropriate support method
 - Plan for future adjustability if needed
 - Calculate proper shelf thickness

2. Fixed Shelf Installation
For permanent shelves:

A. Dado Method:
 - Mark dado locations precisely
 - Set up dado blade or router
 - Cut dados to proper depth (typically 1/4" to 3/8")
 - Test fit shelf pieces
 - Clean dados thoroughly before assembly

B. Cleat Method:
 - Cut support cleats to size
 - Mark cleat positions
 - Pre-drill for screws

- Attach cleats ensuring level
- Test fit shelves before final installation

3. Adjustable Shelf Systems
For flexible storage:

A. Pin Hole System:
  - Create drilling template
  - Mark hole centers
  - Drill holes to consistent depth
  - Clean holes of debris
  - Test pin fit and alignment

B. Track System:
  - Mark track locations
  - Pre-drill mounting holes
  - Install tracks ensuring plumb
  - Check bracket fit
  - Verify smooth adjustment

4. Shelf Construction
Building strong shelves:

A. Solid Wood Shelves:
  - Select straight-grained lumber
  - Edge-glue boards if needed
  - Allow proper curing time

- Sand surfaces thoroughly
- Finish before installation

B. Plywood Shelves:
- Choose appropriate thickness
- Add edge banding if needed
- Cut to final size
- Sand edges smooth
- Apply finish as desired

5. Support Calculations
Understanding load capacity:

A. Weight Distribution:
- Calculate maximum load
- Factor in shelf span
- Consider material strength
- Add safety margin
- Document load limits

B. Support Spacing:
- Determine maximum spans
- Account for material thickness
- Consider load distribution
- Plan support locations
- Verify structural integrity

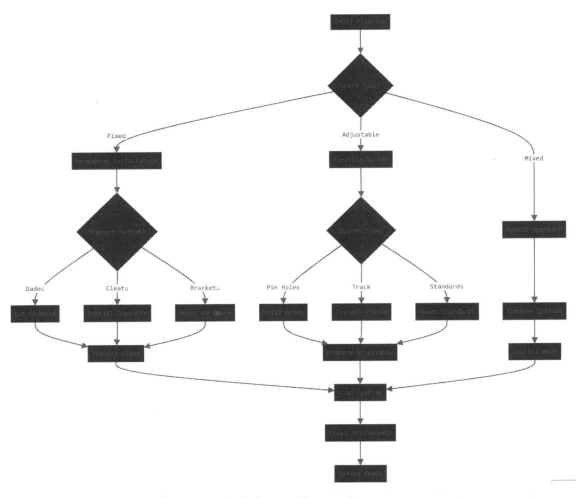

Shelf Support Systems

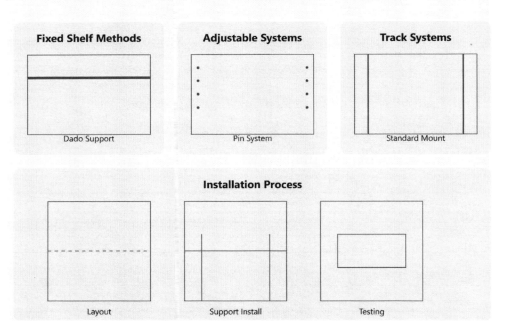

Fixed Shelf Methods	Adjustable Systems	Track Systems
Dado Support	Pin System	Standard Mount

Installation Process

Layout · Support Install · Testing

Surface Preparation and Finishing

Let me guide you through the critical process of surface preparation and finishing. Think of this stage as similar to painting a house - just as a beautiful paint job requires proper wall preparation, a stunning wood finish demands careful surface preparation. The quality of your preparation work directly determines the beauty and durability of your final finish.

Understanding Surface Preparation Fundamentals

Before we apply any finish, we need to understand how wood surfaces interact with finishing materials. Think of wood grain as tiny valleys and ridges - our goal is to smooth these consistently while maintaining the wood's natural beauty. This process involves multiple steps, each building upon the previous one to create an ideal surface for finishing.

For example, when we sand wood, we're not just making it smooth - we're actually cutting the wood fibers at progressively finer levels, creating an optimal surface for finish absorption. This is why proper grit progression is so crucial to achieving professional results.

Systematic Surface Preparation Process

Let's walk through each stage of surface preparation and finishing:

1. Initial Surface Assessment

Begin by carefully evaluating your surface:
- Examine wood grain direction and pattern
- Identify any defects or damage
- Note areas requiring special attention
- Check for old finish residue
- Document problem areas

2. Surface Preparation Sequence

Follow this progression for optimal results:

A. Coarse Sanding (60-80 grit):
- Remove major surface defects
- Level uneven areas
- Sand with the grain
- Check progress frequently
- Remove all dust between grits

B. Medium Sanding (120-150 grit):
- Remove coarse sanding marks
- Continue leveling surface
- Maintain consistent pressure

- Check work under good lighting
- Clean surface thoroughly

C. Fine Sanding (220 grit):
- Create final smooth surface
- Remove medium grit marks
- Prepare for finish application
- Verify surface consistency
- Final cleaning

3. Finish Application Process
Apply finish in controlled conditions:

A. Environment Preparation:
- Control temperature (65-75°F ideal)
- Manage humidity (40-60% optimal)
- Ensure dust-free workspace
- Provide adequate ventilation
- Maintain consistent lighting

B. Application Technique:
- Apply thin, even coats
- Follow grain direction
- Maintain wet edge
- Allow proper drying time
- Sand between coats as needed

4. Quality Control Steps
Maintain high standards throughout:

A. Surface Inspection:
 - Use raking light
 - Check for missed spots
 - Verify consistency
 - Document any issues
 - Make necessary corrections

B. Between-Coat Procedures:
 - Allow full drying time
 - Light scuff sanding
 - Remove all dust
 - Check for defects
 - Maintain clean environment

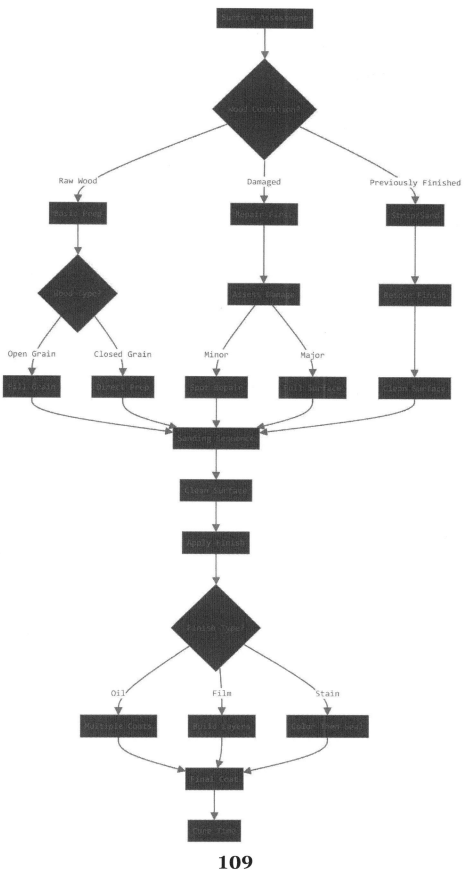

Surface Preparation Guide

Sanding Progression

Coarse (80 grit)

Medium (120 grit)

Fine (220 grit)

Common Defects

Repair Methods

Finish Application

Layer Building

Finishing Process

Surface Prep

Finish Build

Final Inspection

Chapter 5
Mastering Drawer Construction

Drawer Box Construction Methods

Let me guide you through the intricate process of drawer box construction, a fundamental skill in cabinetmaking that combines precision, strength, and functionality. Think of a drawer box as a miniature cabinet that must withstand daily use while sliding smoothly and maintaining its shape. Just as a well-designed car needs both structural integrity and smooth operation, a drawer needs careful construction to provide years of reliable service.

Understanding Drawer Box Construction Fundamentals

Before diving into construction methods, let's understand the key elements that make a successful drawer. A drawer box consists of five main components working together: the front, back, two sides, and bottom. Each piece must be precisely cut and joined to create a box that's not just strong, but also perfectly square and sized to allow smooth operation within the cabinet opening.

When we discuss drawer construction, we're essentially talking about creating a box that must meet three critical requirements: structural integrity to handle loads, precise geometry for smooth operation, and appropriate clearances for easy movement. Let's explore how different construction methods achieve these goals.

Comprehensive Drawer Construction Process

Let me walk you through the systematic process of building a drawer box, explaining each step in detail:

1. Material Selection and Preparation
First, we need to carefully select and prepare our materials:

When choosing wood for drawer sides, consider that different species offer varying benefits. For example, hard maple provides excellent wear resistance and maintains smooth operation, while Baltic birch plywood offers dimensional stability and consistent thickness. The material you select should balance durability, cost, and aesthetic requirements.

The preparation process involves:
 - Milling stock to consistent thickness (typically 1/2" to 5/8" for sides)
 - Squaring edges perfectly for precise joints

- Cutting pieces to final width while maintaining grain orientation
- Allowing wood to acclimate to shop conditions

2. Layout and Marking
Accurate layout is crucial for successful drawer construction:

Think of this phase as creating a detailed roadmap for your cuts. Begin by establishing reference faces and edges on all pieces. These references will guide every subsequent operation and ensure your drawer comes together precisely.

The marking process includes:
- Marking all pieces for orientation
- Laying out joinery locations
- Planning for bottom panel grooves
- Accounting for slide clearances
- Double-checking all measurements

3. Cutting Joinery
The joinery phase requires patience and precision:

Whether you're cutting dovetails, box joints, or rabbets, the process must be methodical. Think of each joint as a puzzle piece that must fit perfectly with its mate. Test cuts on scrap material help dial in settings before cutting your actual drawer parts.

Follow this sequence:
- Set up and test cutting tools
- Cut all similar operations at once
- Maintain consistent pressure
- Check fits after each cut
- Make any necessary adjustments

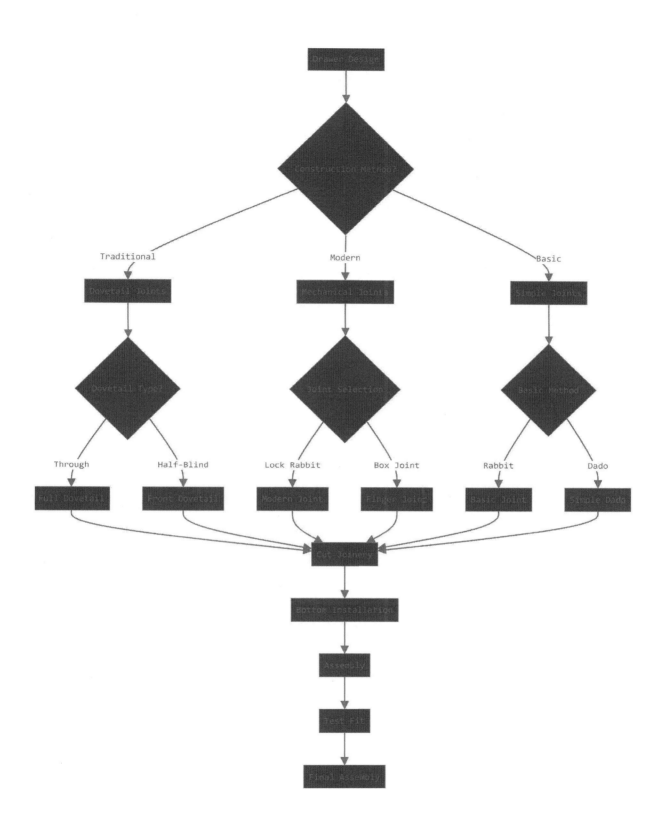

Drawer Construction Guide

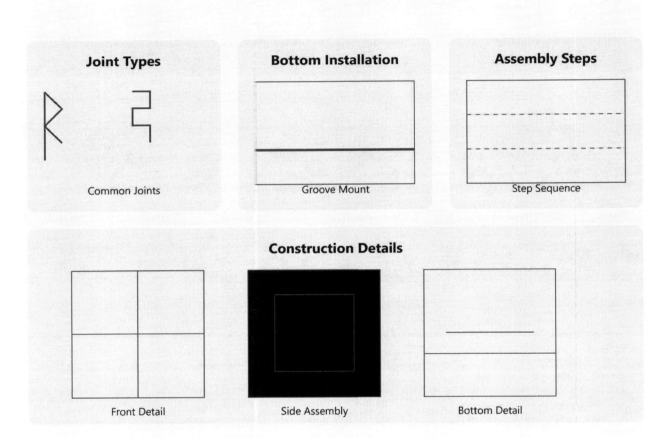

Joint Types

Common Joints

Bottom Installation

Groove Mount

Assembly Steps

Step Sequence

Construction Details

Front Detail

Side Assembly

Bottom Detail

Installing Drawer Slides

Let me guide you through the detailed process of installing drawer slides, a crucial skill that determines how well your drawers will function. Think of drawer slides as the suspension system of a car - just as a vehicle's suspension ensures smooth movement and proper alignment, drawer slides must be installed with precision to provide reliable, smooth operation throughout years of use.

Understanding Drawer Slide Mechanics

Before we begin installation, it's essential to understand how drawer slides work. A typical ball-bearing slide consists of three main components: the cabinet member (attaches to the cabinet), the drawer member (attaches to the drawer), and the intermediate member (contains the ball bearings). These components work together like a well-orchestrated machine, each playing a vital role in smooth drawer operation.

Systematic Installation Process

Let me walk you through the detailed process of installing drawer slides:

1. Preparation and Planning
Begin with thorough preparation:

A. Cabinet Preparation:
  - Clean all mounting surfaces
  - Check cabinet for square
  - Verify internal dimensions
  - Mark reference lines
  - Install blocking if needed

B. Drawer Preparation:
  - Confirm drawer dimensions
  - Check drawer square
  - Verify clearances
  - Mark mounting locations
  - Pre-drill if necessary

2. Layout and Marking
Accurate layout is crucial:

A. Cabinet Layout:
  - Measure from cabinet front
  - Mark setback distance
  - Use story stick for multiple drawers
  - Mark vertical locations
  - Double-check all measurements

B. Drawer Layout:
  - Mark centerlines
  - Indicate mounting holes

- Account for overlay or inset
- Mark slide locations
- Verify symmetry

3. Mounting Sequence
Follow a systematic approach:

A. Cabinet Member Installation:
- Position slide accurately
- Level horizontally
- Secure front screw
- Check for plumb
- Install remaining screws

B. Drawer Member Installation:
- Position on drawer
- Align with reference marks
- Secure front screw
- Check alignment
- Complete attachment

4. Testing and Adjustment
Ensure proper operation:

A. Initial Testing:
- Insert drawer carefully
- Check smooth operation

- Verify equal gaps
- Test full extension
- Listen for proper rolling

B. Fine Adjustments:
- Adjust height if needed
- Set side clearances
- Check stop positions
- Verify self-closing
- Test load capacity

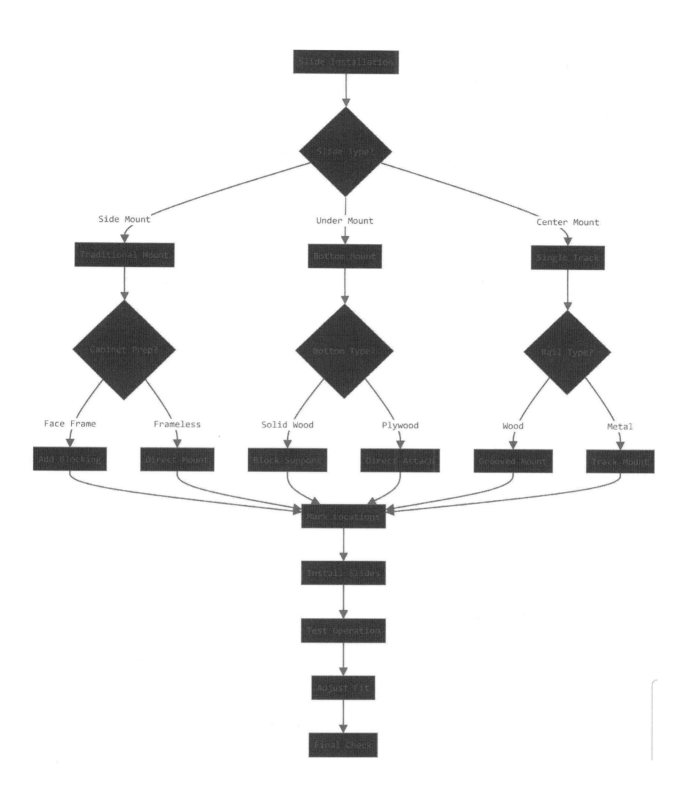

Custom Drawer Sizing Guide

Clearance Requirements

Side Clearances

Height Calculations

Height Components

Component Layout

Part Relationships

Measurement Process

Opening Check

Clearance Calc

Final Dimensions

Creating Custom-Sized Drawers

Let me walk you through the intricate process of creating custom-sized drawers, a skill that combines precise measurement, careful planning, and attention to detail. Think of this process as similar to tailoring a suit - just as a tailor must consider both the wearer's measurements and the fabric's properties, we must account for both the cabinet opening and our materials' characteristics to create drawers that fit and function perfectly.

Understanding Drawer Sizing Fundamentals

Before we begin calculating dimensions, it's essential to understand how a drawer's various components work together. A perfectly sized drawer requires careful consideration of multiple clearances and relationships:

The drawer box must be narrower than the cabinet opening to allow for smooth operation. Like a train needs clearance in its tunnel, a drawer needs specific clearances on each side for proper movement. These clearances vary based on your chosen slide type and installation method.

Height calculations must account for both the drawer box construction and any overlay or inset requirements of your drawer front.

Similar to how a picture frame needs precise measurements to display its contents properly, drawer fronts must be sized to create consistent reveals and proper coverage.

Comprehensive Sizing Process

Let me guide you through the detailed process of calculating and creating custom drawer sizes:

1. Initial Measurements
Begin with precise opening measurements:

Think of this step as creating a detailed map of your available space. Just as an architect must understand the building site before designing, we need to thoroughly understand our cabinet opening before determining drawer dimensions.

The process involves:
 - Measuring width at multiple points (front, middle, back)
 - Checking height at several locations
 - Verifying depth is consistent
 - Checking for square
 - Noting any irregularities

2. Clearance Calculations
Determine necessary clearances based on hardware:

Consider this like calculating the safety margins in engineering. Just as a bridge needs specific clearances for different types of traffic, drawers need specific clearances based on their hardware and use.

For example:
 - Side-mount slides typically require 1/2" to 1" total width reduction
 - Under-mount slides need specific bottom clearance
 - Height clearances vary by slide manufacturer
 - Additional clearance may be needed for drawer front adjustability

3. Box Construction Planning
Plan your drawer box dimensions:

Similar to planning the framing of a house, we need to account for how all components will fit together. Different construction methods require different allowances:

For traditional dovetail construction:
- Account for pin and tail depth
- Allow for bottom panel groove
- Consider material thickness

- Plan for front/back setback
- Calculate overall dimensions

For modern mechanical joints:
- Account for joint overlap
- Allow for bottom installation
- Consider hardware requirements
- Plan for slide attachment
- Verify final measurements

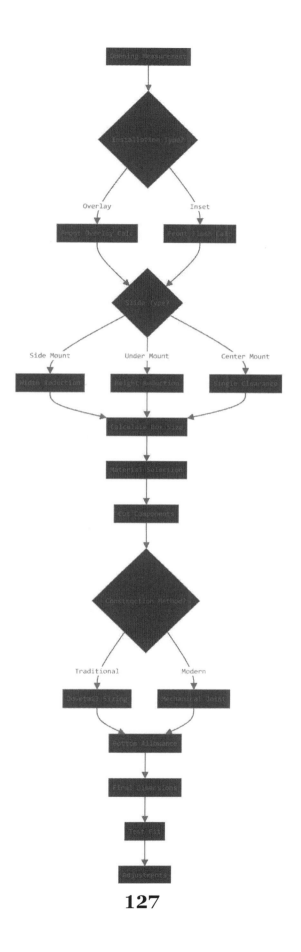

Custom Drawer Sizing Guide

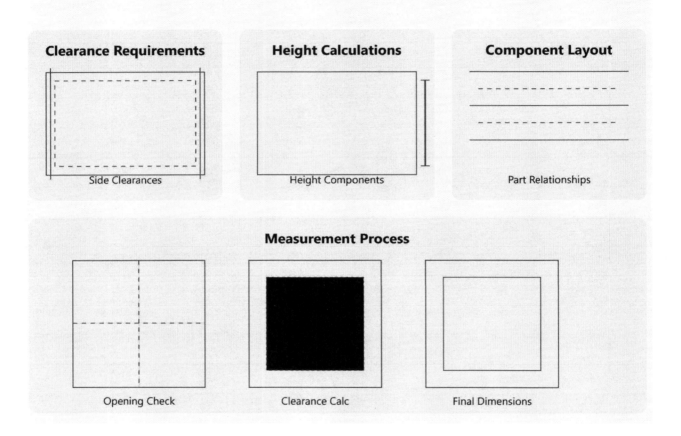

Clearance Requirements

Side Clearances

Height Calculations

Height Components

Component Layout

Part Relationships

Measurement Process

Opening Check

Clearance Calc

Final Dimensions

Drawer Front Installation and Alignment

Let me guide you through the precise process of installing and aligning drawer fronts, a crucial step that transforms a functional drawer box into a visually appealing and professionally finished piece. Think of this process as similar to hanging a gallery of paintings - just as each artwork needs to be perfectly level and properly spaced from its neighbors, each drawer front must be precisely positioned to create consistent reveals and proper alignment with adjacent elements.

Understanding Drawer Front Relationships

Before we dive into installation, we need to understand how drawer fronts relate to surrounding elements. Just as a musical conductor must ensure each instrument plays in harmony with the others, we must ensure each drawer front works in concert with adjacent cabinet elements to create a cohesive visual presentation.

The key relationships include:
The reveal (the visible gap between elements) must be consistent around all edges, much like the spacing between words on a page. This spacing creates visual rhythm and indicates professional-level craftsmanship.

The alignment must be perfect in multiple planes - imagine a grid overlaid on your cabinet front. Each drawer front should align perfectly with this grid while maintaining proper reveals with adjacent elements.

Systematic Installation Process

Let me walk you through the detailed process of installing and aligning drawer fronts:

1. Preparation and Planning
Begin with thorough preparation. Just as a chef mise en place ensures all ingredients are ready before cooking, we must have all our components and tools prepared before beginning installation:

First, prepare your workspace and materials:
  - Clean all surfaces thoroughly
  - Gather necessary tools and hardware
  - Prepare temporary spacers for reveals
  - Set up lighting for good visibility
  - Ensure adequate working space

Then, organize your mounting hardware:
  - Sort mounting brackets or screws
  - Prepare drill and drill bits
  - Have measuring tools ready

- Set up clamps if needed
- Prepare pencils for marking

2. Initial Positioning

Think of this step as creating a rough draft. Just as a writer first gets ideas on paper before refining them, we'll establish basic position before fine-tuning:

Start with basic alignment:
- Use spacers for consistent reveals
- Center drawer front on box
- Check vertical alignment
- Verify horizontal level
- Mark reference points

3. Mounting Process

Now we move to securing the drawer front, similar to how a jeweler sets a stone in its mounting:

For direct mounting:
- Mark screw locations carefully
- Pre-drill pilot holes
- Use proper screw size
- Don't fully tighten yet
- Allow for adjustment

For bracket mounting:
- Install brackets on box
- Attach front brackets
- Make initial connections
- Leave slightly loose
- Verify operation

4. Fine Adjustment

This critical phase requires patience and precision:

Consider these relationships:
- Vertical alignment with adjacent drawers
- Horizontal reveal consistency
- Face alignment with cabinet
- Operation clearance
- Overall visual balance

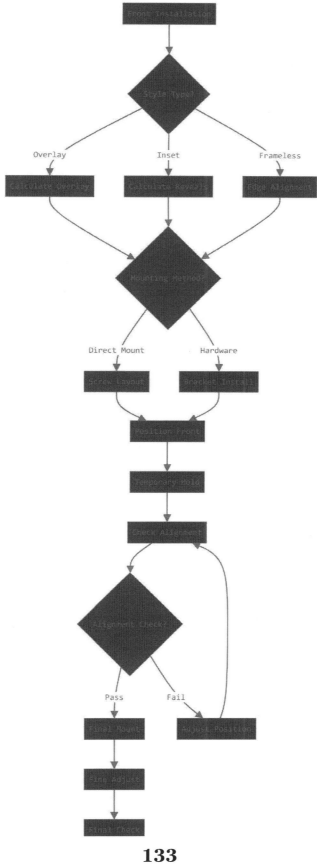

Drawer Front Alignment Guide

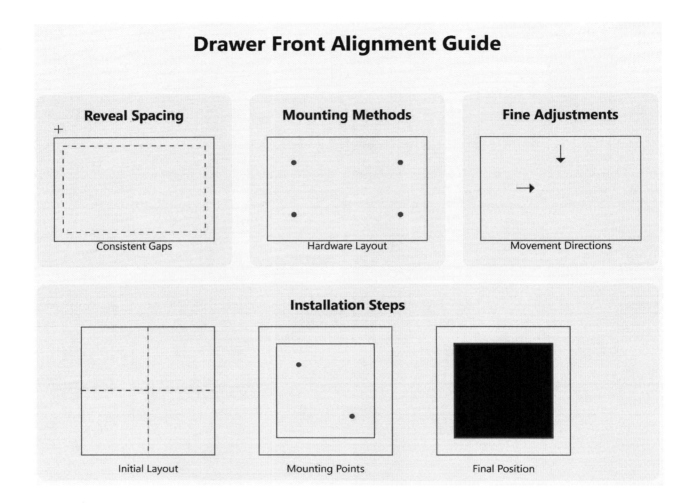

Reveal Spacing
Consistent Gaps

Mounting Methods
Hardware Layout

Fine Adjustments
Movement Directions

Installation Steps

Initial Layout

Mounting Points

Final Position

Chapter 6
Door Making and Installation

Types of Cabinet Doors

Let me guide you through the fascinating world of cabinet door styles and construction methods. Think of cabinet doors as the face of your project - just as architectural facades define a building's character, cabinet doors set the tone for your entire piece. Each door type has its own personality and construction challenges, much like how different architectural styles require specific building techniques.

Understanding Cabinet Door Fundamentals

Cabinet doors can be categorized into three main families, each with its own construction methods and visual characteristics:

Slab doors are like a canvas - a single, solid piece that can be either understated or dramatic depending on the wood selection and edge treatment. Think of them as the modernist approach to door design, where simplicity and material quality take center stage.

Frame and panel doors are like a picture frame holding a canvas. The frame provides stability while allowing the panel to move with seasonal changes, much like how a floating floor system allows for movement while maintaining structural integrity.

Detailed Door Type Analysis

Let me walk you through each major door type and its characteristics:

1. Slab Doors
The simplest form can be the most challenging to execute well:

The Construction Process involves:
- Material selection: Choose stable wood or engineered materials
- Panel glue-up: Careful grain matching and joining
- Edge treatment: Consider durability and aesthetics
- Surface preparation: Thorough sanding and finishing
- Hardware preparation: Precise hinge and pull locations

Key Considerations include:
- Wood movement across the width
- Grain direction for stability
- Edge detail impact on appearance

- Surface flatness maintenance
- Hardware mounting strength

2. Frame and Panel Doors

These traditional doors offer proven reliability:

The Frame Construction requires:
- Stile and rail dimensioning
- Joint selection (mortise and tenon, dowel, etc.)
- Panel groove sizing
- Panel float allowance
- Assembly sequence planning

Panel Options include:
- Raised panel (traditional)
- Flat panel (contemporary)
- Beaded panel (decorative)
- Glass panel (display)
- Wire mesh or metal (industrial)

3. Mixed Style Doors

Modern interpretations of classical designs:

Design Elements combine:
- Frame widths and proportions
- Panel treatments and profiles
- Edge details and reveals
- Material combinations

- Hardware integration

Construction Considerations include:
- Material compatibility
- Joint strength requirements
- Movement accommodation
- Finish matching
- Installation methods

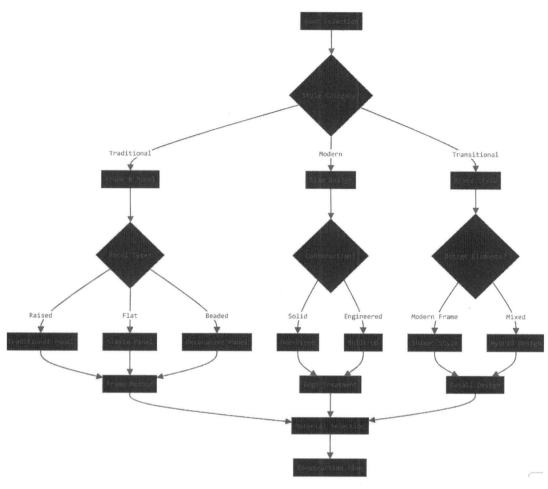

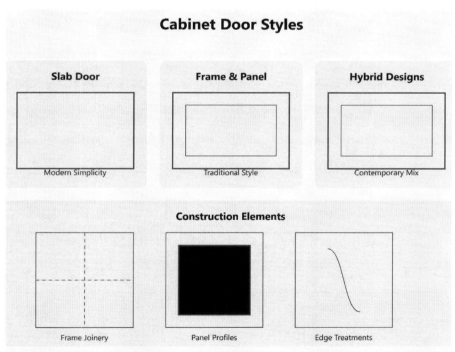

Cabinet Door Styles

Slab Door

Modern Simplicity

Frame & Panel

Traditional Style

Hybrid Designs

Contemporary Mix

Construction Elements

Frame Joinery

Panel Profiles

Edge Treatments

139

Frame-and-Panel Door Construction

Let me walk you through the intricate process of constructing frame-and-panel doors, a time-tested method that combines beauty with practical function. Imagine building a picture frame that not only looks beautiful but must also operate smoothly while accommodating natural wood movement. Just as a bridge must flex with temperature changes without losing its strength, a frame-and-panel door must allow its panel to expand and contract through seasonal changes while maintaining its structural integrity.

Understanding Frame-and-Panel Construction Principles

Think of a frame-and-panel door as a sophisticated system of interlocking components. The frame, consisting of stiles (vertical members) and rails (horizontal members), creates a strong perimeter that resists warping. Within this frame floats the panel, like a sheet of paper held loosely in a picture frame, able to move slightly as humidity changes without causing stress to the overall structure.

This design has endured for centuries because it solves a fundamental woodworking challenge: wood's natural tendency to expand and contract across its width. By allowing the panel to float freely within the frame's grooves, this movement is accommodated without compromising the door's appearance or function.

Comprehensive Construction Process

Let me guide you through the detailed process of building a frame-and-panel door:

1. Material Selection and Preparation
Just as a chef selects the finest ingredients for a special dish, we must choose our materials carefully:

For the frame:
 - Select straight-grained, stable wood
 - Choose quarter-sawn material if possible
 - Mill stock slightly oversized
 - Allow wood to acclimate
 - Mark reference faces and edges

For the panel:
 - Consider wood movement direction
 - Select matching grain patterns
 - Account for raised panel requirements
 - Plan for proper thickness
 - Allow extra material for testing

2. Component Layout and Cutting
Think of this stage as creating a precise map of your door:

Frame components:
 - Calculate stile lengths   **141**

- Determine rail widths
- Plan joint locations
- Consider reveals and overlays
- Account for groove depths

Panel sizing:
- Calculate panel dimensions
- Allow for seasonal movement
- Consider raise height if applicable
- Plan grain orientation
- Account for groove depth

3. Joint Creation
This critical phase requires careful attention to detail:

For mortise and tenon joints:
- Lay out mortise locations
- Set up mortising tools
- Cut mortises to proper depth
- Create matching tenons
- Test fit each joint

For the panel groove:
- Set up groove cutting tool
- Maintain consistent depth
- Ensure proper width
- Check groove alignment
- Test panel fit

142

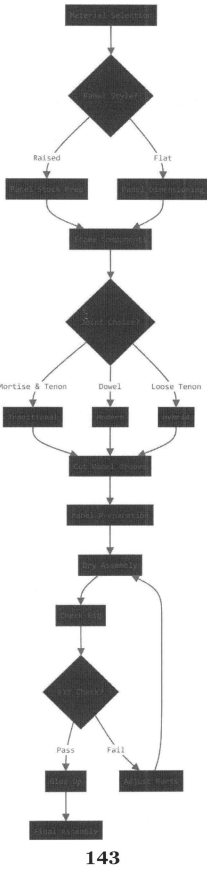

Frame-and-Panel Construction

Joint Details

Mortise and Tenon

Panel Profiles

Panel Types

Assembly View

Component Layout

Assembly Sequence

Stock Preparation

Joint Cutting

Final Assembly

Installing Hinges

Let me guide you through the intricate process of hinge installation, a critical skill that determines how well your cabinet doors will function. Think of hinges as the joints in a dancer's body - just as a dancer needs properly functioning joints for graceful movement, a cabinet door needs correctly installed hinges for smooth, reliable operation.

Understanding Hinge Types and Their Requirements

Before we begin installation, it's essential to understand how different hinges work. Picture hinges as tiny machines, each type with its own specific requirements for positioning and adjustment. Just as different door types need different hinges, each hinge type needs its own particular installation approach.

Systematic Installation Process

Let me guide you through the detailed process of installing hinges, breaking down each critical step:

1. Preparation Phase
Start with thorough planning and setup:

First, gather your materials and tools:
  - Selected hinges and mounting hardware
  - Appropriate templates or jigs
  - Sharp marking tools
  - Precise measuring instruments
  - Required cutting tools
  - Drill and bits if needed

Then, prepare your work area:
  - Clean, well-lit workspace
  - Sturdy work surface
  - Protected door surfaces
  - Easy access to tools
  - Good ventilation for mortising

2. Layout and Marking
Precision here prevents problems later:

For Traditional Hinges:
  - Mark hinge locations carefully
  - Use story stick for multiple doors
  - Transfer marks accurately
  - Double-check measurements
  - Consider reveal requirements

For European Hinges:
  - Layout cup locations
  - Mark mounting plate positions
  - Account for overlays
  - Consider adjustability needs
  - Verify clearances

3. Mortising Process (if required)

Execute this crucial step carefully:

Mortise Preparation:
  - Set up templates or guides
  - Secure workpiece firmly
  - Choose appropriate tools
  - Make test cuts on scrap
  - Verify mortise depth

Cutting Sequence:
  - Start with outline scoring
  - Remove bulk material
  - Clean mortise corners
  - Test fit frequently
  - Maintain consistent depth

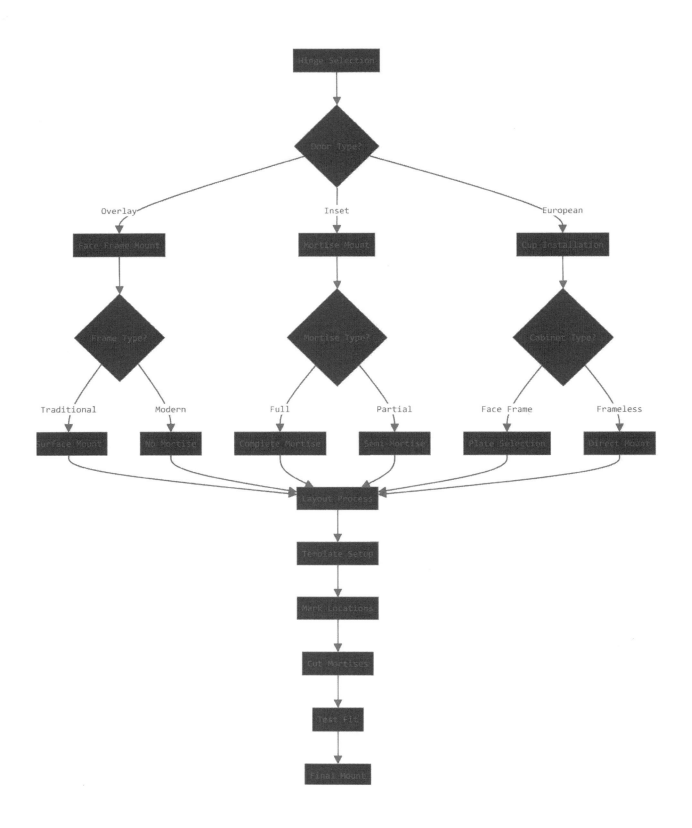

Hinge Installation Guide

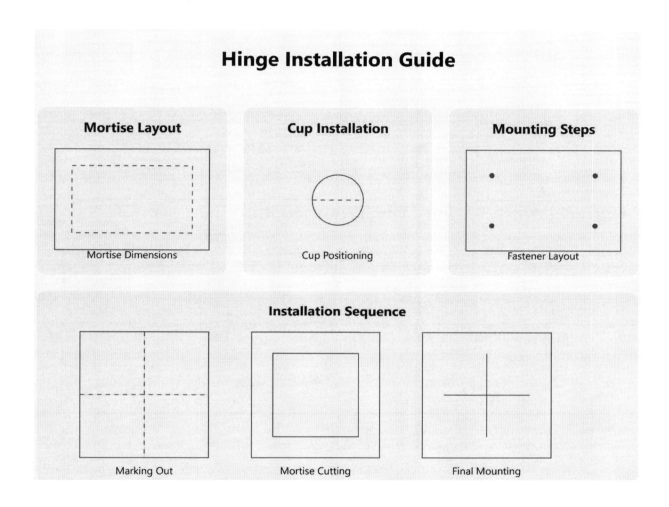

Mortise Layout
Mortise Dimensions

Cup Installation
Cup Positioning

Mounting Steps
Fastener Layout

Installation Sequence
Marking Out

Mortise Cutting

Final Mounting

Door Alignment and Adjustment

Let me guide you through the intricate process of door alignment and adjustment, a skill that transforms a basic installation into a professionally finished project. Think of cabinet door adjustment as similar to tuning a fine musical instrument - just as a piano requires precise adjustments to create perfect harmony, cabinet doors need careful alignment to create visual harmony and smooth operation.

Understanding Door Alignment Principles

Before we begin adjustments, we need to understand how doors relate to their surroundings. Imagine your cabinet face as a grid system where every gap and reveal must be consistent, like the spacing between words on a printed page. These relationships create the visual harmony that marks professional-quality work.

Three key dimensions must be considered: up-and-down (vertical), side-to-side (horizontal), and in-and-out (depth). Like adjusting a three-dimensional puzzle, changes in one direction often affect the others, requiring a systematic approach to achieve perfect alignment.

Systematic Adjustment Process

Let me walk you through the comprehensive process of adjusting cabinet doors:

1. Initial Assessment
Begin with a thorough evaluation of the current situation:

First, examine the overall appearance:
- Check reveal consistency
- Verify door alignment with cabinet face
- Look for parallel edges
- Assess gaps between doors
- Note any binding points

Then, test door operation:
- Open and close fully
- Listen for rubbing sounds
- Feel for smooth movement
- Check self-closing function
- Verify proper latching

2. Systematic Adjustment
Address issues in a specific order:

Vertical Adjustment:
- Start with height alignment

- Set equal top and bottom reveals
- Check adjacent door relationships
- Verify cabinet face alignment
- Test door operation

Horizontal Adjustment:
- Adjust side-to-side position
- Create consistent side reveals
- Align multiple door edges
- Check for parallel gaps
- Verify proper clearances

Depth Adjustment:
- Set door face alignment
- Adjust for proper overlay
- Check face alignment between doors
- Verify proper closure
- Test operation clearance

3. Fine-Tuning Process
Make precise adjustments:

For European Hinges:
- Use adjustment screws systematically
- Make small incremental changes
- Check results after each adjustment
- maintain proper tension
- Document final settings   **152**

For Traditional Hinges:
- Loosen mounting screws slightly
- Make position adjustments
- Use shims if needed
- Retighten progressively
- Verify stability

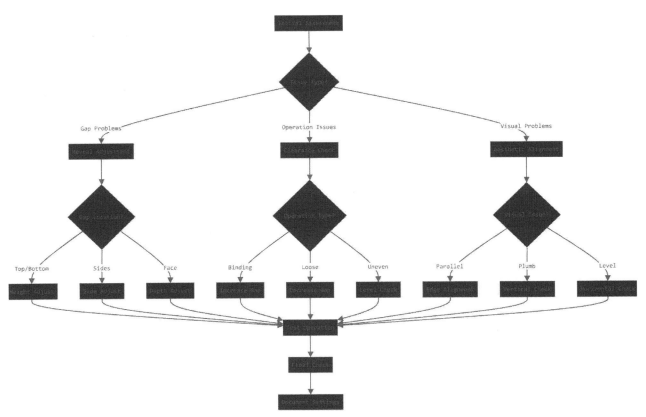

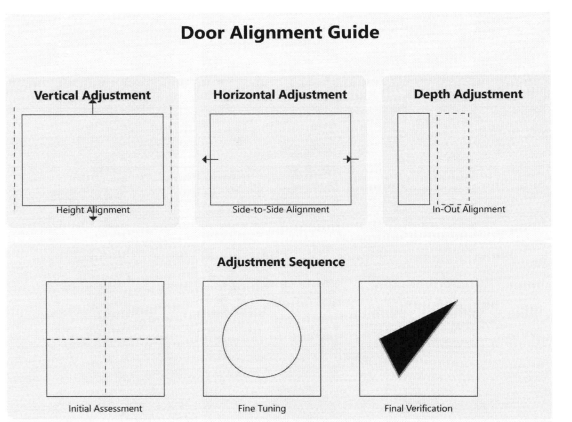

Door Alignment Guide

Vertical Adjustment
Height Alignment

Horizontal Adjustment
Side-to-Side Alignment

Depth Adjustment
In-Out Alignment

Adjustment Sequence

Initial Assessment

Fine Tuning

Final Verification

PART III
ADVANCED PROJECTS

Chapter 7
Workshop Storage Solutions

Tool Cabinet Construction

Let me guide you through the process of building a comprehensive tool cabinet - think of it as creating a custom home for each of your valued workshop tools. Just as a well-designed house needs careful planning to serve its inhabitants perfectly, a tool cabinet requires thoughtful design to protect and organize your tools while making them easily accessible.

Understanding Tool Cabinet Design Principles

A well-designed tool cabinet is like a small workshop within your workshop. Consider how each morning, you'll open this cabinet to begin your day's work. Every tool should be immediately visible and accessible, yet protected from dust and damage. The cabinet's organization should reflect your natural workflow, with frequently used tools placed at comfortable heights and grouped by function.

Think about how tools relate to each other in your work process. Just as a kitchen organizes ingredients near the prep area and cooking utensils near the stove, your tool cabinet should group related tools together: measuring and marking tools in one zone, cutting tools in another, and so forth.
```

## Comprehensive Construction Process

Let me walk you through the detailed process of building a tool cabinet, breaking down each crucial phase:

1. Planning and Design Phase
Begin with thorough assessment and planning:

First, inventory your tools:
  - Measure each tool's dimensions
  - Group tools by function
  - Note frequency of use
  - Consider future additions
  - Plan for special storage needs

Then, design the cabinet:
  - Determine overall dimensions
  - Plan interior divisions
  - Choose door style
  - Design tool holders
```

- Account for lighting needs

2. Cabinet Construction
Build from the outside in:

Cabinet Box:
- Select appropriate materials
- Cut components to size
- Create strong joints
- Install back panel
- Add reinforcement where needed

Interior Framework:
- Build internal dividers
- Install shelf supports
- Create tool holding systems
- Add adjustable elements
- Plan for future modifications

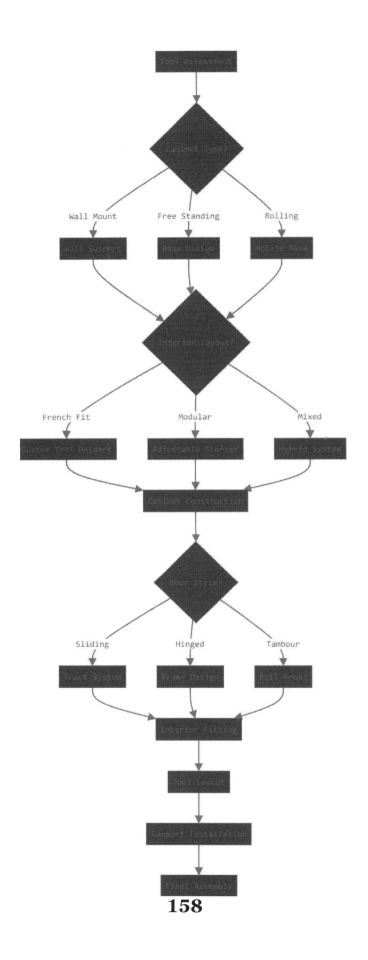

Tool Cabinet Design Guide

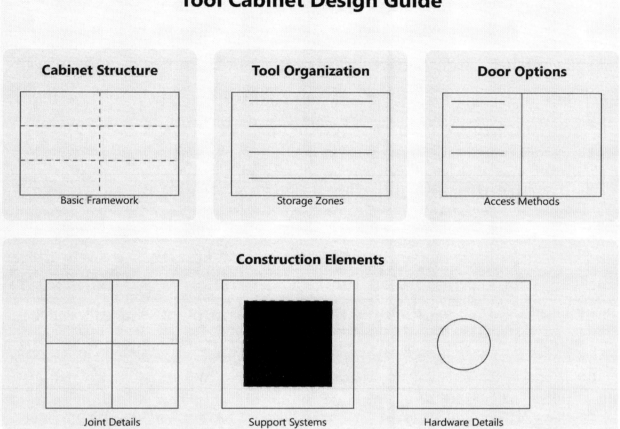

Cabinet Structure

Basic Framework

Tool Organization

Storage Zones

Door Options

Access Methods

Construction Elements

Joint Details

Support Systems

Hardware Details

Mobile Storage Carts

Let me guide you through the process of creating mobile storage carts that combine flexibility with functionality. Think of a mobile storage cart as a workshop assistant that brings tools and materials exactly where you need them. Just as a well-trained assistant anticipates your needs and moves efficiently, a well-designed cart should organize materials logically and move smoothly through your workspace.

Understanding Mobile Cart Design Principles

Before we begin construction, let's understand what makes a mobile cart truly functional. Consider the cart's primary purpose - like a specialized vehicle, it must be stable enough to carry heavy loads while remaining maneuverable in tight spaces. The design must balance weight distribution, accessibility, and storage capacity.

Think about how you'll use the cart in your daily workflow. Just as a chef's cart places frequently used ingredients within easy reach, your mobile cart should position commonly used items at convenient heights and make them easily accessible from multiple sides.

Systematic Construction Process

Let me walk you through the detailed process of building a mobile storage cart, explaining each crucial step:

1. Planning and Design Phase
Just as an architect begins with careful planning, we'll start by defining our cart's requirements:

First, assess your needs:
  - Determine primary cart function
  - List items to be stored
  - Calculate weight requirements
  - Consider workspace constraints
  - Plan access requirements

Then, design the cart:
  - Sketch basic dimensions
  - Plan storage configurations
  - Choose wheel/caster type
  - Design work surfaces
  - Plan material requirements

2. Base Construction
The foundation of your cart must be rock-solid:

Frame Assembly:
  - Cut base frame members **161**

- Create strong corner joints
- Install cross bracing
- Add caster mounting plates
- Level and square the base

3. Storage Integration
Build up from your solid foundation:

For Drawer Systems:
  - Install drawer slides
  - Build drawer boxes
  - Add dividers and organizers
  - Install drawer fronts
  - Test smooth operation

For Shelf Systems:
  - Add vertical supports
  - Install shelf cleats
  - Create adjustable options
  - Add edge protection
  - Install safety features

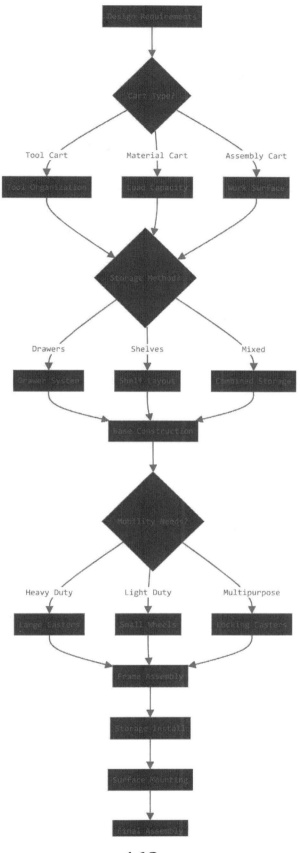

Mobile Cart Design Guide

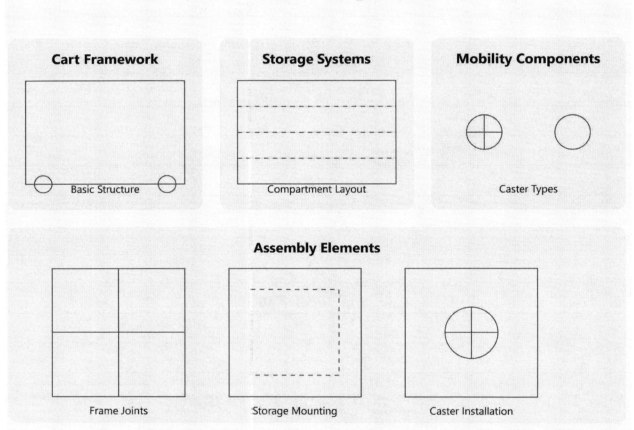

Cart Framework

Basic Structure

Storage Systems

Compartment Layout

Mobility Components

Caster Types

Assembly Elements

Frame Joints

Storage Mounting

Caster Installation

Wall-Mounted Organization Systems

Let me guide you through the process of creating wall-mounted organization systems, a crucial skill for maximizing workshop space. Think of your workshop walls as valuable real estate - just as cities build upward when ground space is limited, workshops can dramatically increase storage capacity by effectively using vertical space.

Understanding Wall Organization Fundamentals

Before we begin installation, we need to understand how wall-mounted systems distribute load. Consider the wall as a load-bearing foundation - just as a building's foundation must support its entire weight, your wall system needs proper support to safely hold tools and materials. Every component, from the mounting cleats to the individual tool holders, plays a vital role in creating a secure and functional system.

Comprehensive Installation Process

Let me guide you through the detailed process of creating a wall-mounted organization system, breaking down each crucial phase:

1. Wall Assessment and Preparation

Before mounting anything, we need to thoroughly understand our mounting surface:

Start with structural evaluation:
 - Locate and mark wall studs
 - Assess wall material strength
 - Check for any utilities in the wall
 - Look for potential problem areas
 - Verify load-bearing capacity

Then prepare the mounting area:
 - Clear the wall completely
 - Repair any damage
 - Clean mounting surfaces
 - Establish level lines
 - Mark stud locations clearly

2. Support System Installation

The foundation of your wall system must be rock-solid:

For French Cleat Systems:
 - Cut cleats at precise 45-degree angles
 - Ensure perfectly straight cuts
 - Mount wall cleats into studs
 - Level each cleat carefully
 - Test cleat engagement

For Panel Systems:
  - Install proper anchoring
  - Mount support framework
  - Level and plumb panels
  - Secure all connections
  - Verify panel stability

3. Organization Layout

Think strategically about tool placement:

Consider these factors:
  - Frequency of tool use
  - Tool weight and size
  - Related tool groupings
  - Access requirements
  - Future flexibility needs

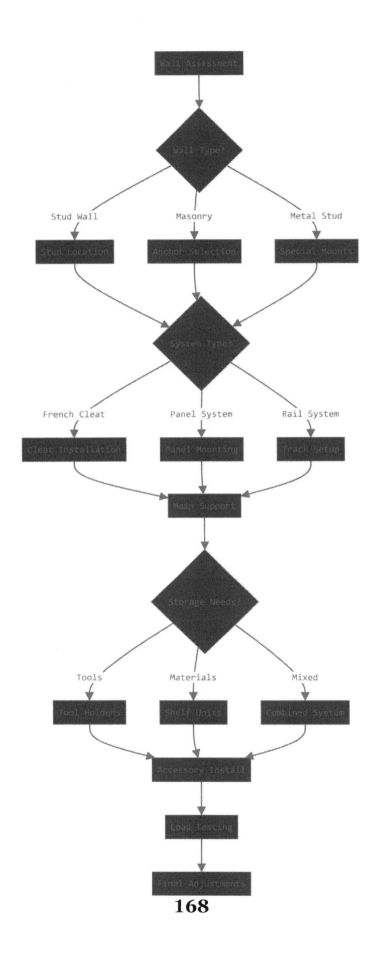

Wall Organization Guide

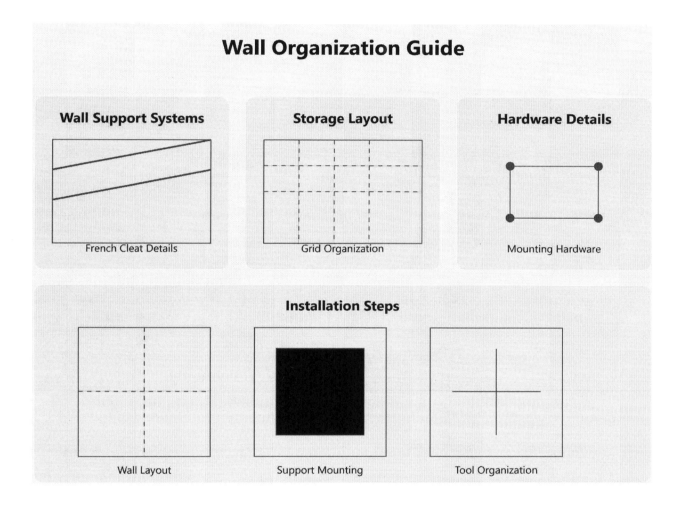

Wall Support Systems

French Cleat Details

Storage Layout

Grid Organization

Hardware Details

Mounting Hardware

Installation Steps

Wall Layout

Support Mounting

Tool Organization

Lumber Storage Solutions

Let me walk you through the process of designing and building an effective lumber storage system. Think of this as creating a specialized library for your wood collection - just as a library needs to protect books while keeping them accessible, a lumber storage system must protect your valuable materials while maintaining easy access.

Understanding Lumber Storage Fundamentals

Before we dive into construction, let's understand the critical principles of proper lumber storage. Imagine your wood as a living, breathing material (because it is!) that needs the right environment to remain stable and usable. Just as wine needs specific storage conditions to maintain its quality, lumber requires proper support, air circulation, and protection from environmental factors.

Comprehensive Construction Process

Let me guide you through the detailed process of building a lumber storage system, breaking down each crucial phase:

1. Space Assessment and Planning
First, we need to evaluate our space and storage needs:

Begin with space analysis:
- Measure available floor space
- Check ceiling height clearance
- Identify optimal wall areas
- Consider traffic patterns
- Evaluate floor load capacity

Then assess storage requirements:
- List typical lumber sizes
- Calculate maximum load weights
- Plan for sheet goods storage
- Consider future expansion
- Account for specialty items

2. Support Structure Design

The foundation of your storage system must be rock-solid:

For vertical storage:
- Design robust wall brackets
- Plan support spacing
- Calculate load distribution
- Include safety features
- Design divider system

For horizontal racks:
- Calculate beam spans
- Design support posts
- Plan level adjustments

171

- Include cross bracing
- Design accessible layout

3. Construction Implementation

Building the system requires careful attention to detail:

Support installation:
- Locate wall studs or structure
- Install proper anchoring
- Level all supports
- Test load capacity
- Add safety features

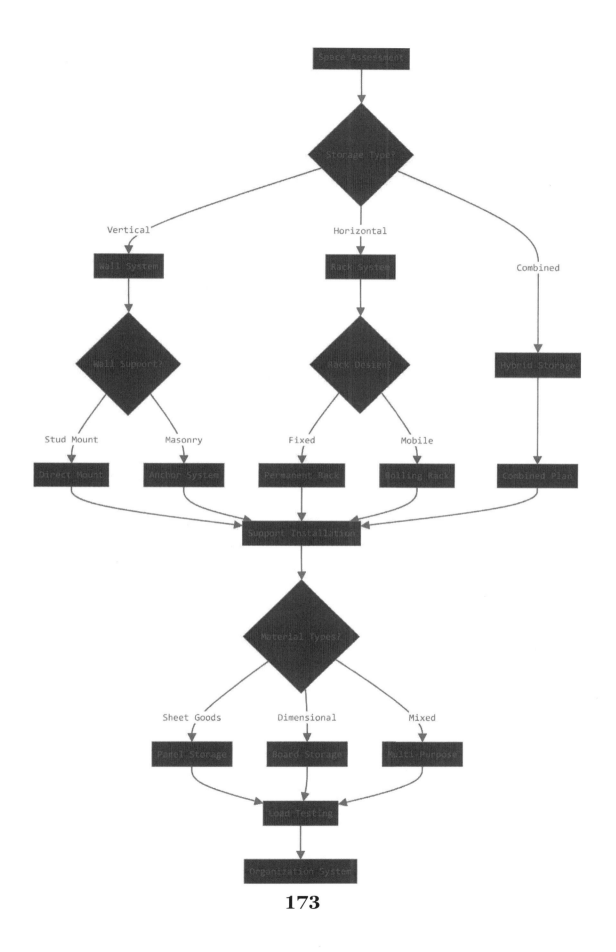

Lumber Storage Design Guide

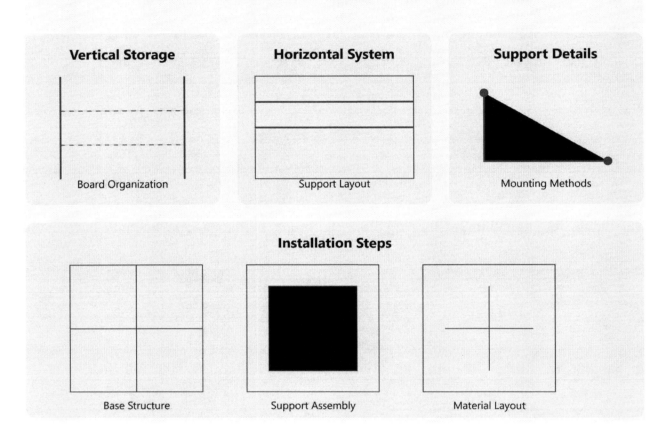

Vertical Storage

Board Organization

Horizontal System

Support Layout

Support Details

Mounting Methods

Installation Steps

Base Structure

Support Assembly

Material Layout

Chapter 8
Home Organization Projects

Closet Organization Systems

Let me guide you through the comprehensive process of designing and building closet organization systems. Think of a closet as a room within a room - like a miniature living space that needs to be perfectly tailored to its contents while maximizing every inch of available space.

Understanding Closet Organization Fundamentals

Before diving into construction, we need to understand how different storage elements work together to create an efficient system. Just as a well-designed kitchen has specific zones for different activities, a well-organized closet needs distinct areas for various types of storage. Each component must work in harmony with others while maximizing the available space.

Systematic Installation Process

Let me guide you through the detailed process of creating a closet organization system, breaking down each crucial phase:

1. Space Assessment and Planning
Begin with thorough evaluation and planning:

Initial Assessment:
- Measure all dimensions precisely
- Note door swing clearances
- Identify wall construction type
- Check for obstacles (vents, switches)
- Consider lighting requirements

Storage Requirements Analysis:
- List all items to be stored
- Measure long hanging items
- Calculate folded item space
- Plan shoe storage needs
- Account for seasonal variations

2. Design Development
Create a comprehensive plan:

Layout Planning:
- Draw to-scale diagrams
- Plan traffic patterns
- Design storage zones
- Consider accessibility
- Allow for future flexibility

Component Selection:
- Choose appropriate shelving
- Select rod types and placement
- Plan drawer configurations
- Design specialty storage
- Include adjustable elements

3. Installation Sequence
Follow a logical order:

Support Structure:
- Locate and mark wall studs
- Install support rails or cleats
- Level all support components
- Verify secure mounting
- Test weight capacity

Closet Organization Guide

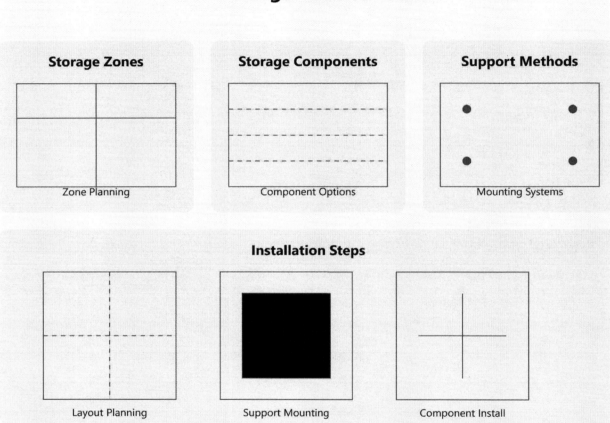

Storage Zones

Zone Planning

Storage Components

Component Options

Support Methods

Mounting Systems

Installation Steps

Layout Planning

Support Mounting

Component Install

Pantry Storage Solutions

Let me guide you through the comprehensive process of designing and building pantry storage solutions. Think of a pantry as a mini grocery store within your home - just as stores organize products for easy access and inventory management, your pantry needs thoughtful organization to make food storage efficient and accessible.

Understanding Pantry Storage Principles

Before we begin construction, consider how a pantry functions in daily life. Like a well-organized library where books are categorized and easily accessible, a pantry needs clear zones for different types of items, with frequently used items at eye level and heavier items lower down. The system must accommodate various container sizes while maintaining visibility and accessibility.

Detailed Implementation Process

Let me walk you through the comprehensive process of creating an efficient pantry storage system:

1. Space Analysis and Planning
Begin with thorough evaluation:

Space Assessment:
- Measure all dimensions precisely
- Note door swing clearances
- Identify light sources
- Check for obstacles (pipes, vents)
- Consider ventilation needs
- Document electrical outlets

Usage Analysis:
- List all storage categories
- Calculate space needs per category
- Consider container sizes
- Plan for bulk storage
- Account for seasonal variations
- Evaluate frequency of access

2. Design Development
Create a functional layout:

Zone Planning:
- Designate specific areas by use
- Plan eye-level access for frequent items
- Position heavy items lower
- Create zones for different categories
- Include space for growth
- Design clear sightlines

180

Component Selection:
- Choose appropriate shelf depths
- Select shelf material thickness
- Plan pull-out systems
- Design corner solutions
- Include specialty storage
- Consider container accessibility

3. Construction Implementation
Build in logical sequence:

Support Structure:
- Install wall cleats
- Mount vertical standards
- Level all components
- Secure support brackets
- Test weight capacity
- Verify stability

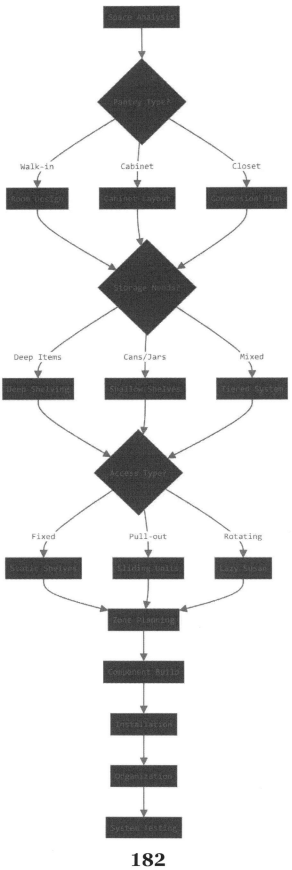

Pantry Storage Design Guide

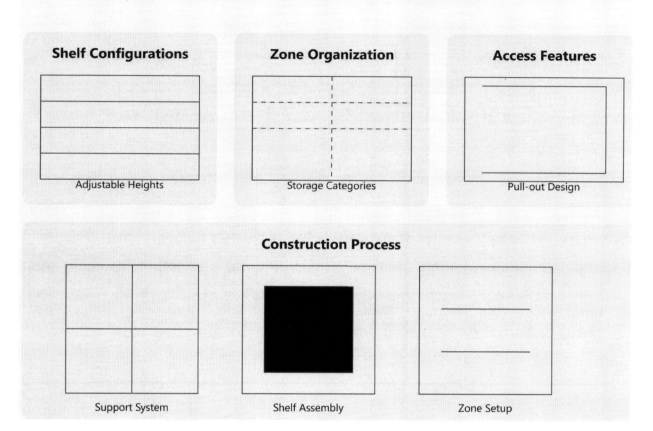

Shelf Configurations

Adjustable Heights

Zone Organization

Storage Categories

Access Features

Pull-out Design

Construction Process

Support System

Shelf Assembly

Zone Setup

Mudroom Storage Units

Let me guide you through the process of creating effective mudroom storage solutions - think of a mudroom as your home's airlock, a transitional space that needs to efficiently handle the chaos of daily comings and goings while keeping the rest of your home clean and organized.

Understanding Mudroom Storage Fundamentals

Picture your mudroom as a personal locker room for each family member. Just as professional sports teams need organized spaces for equipment and gear, families need well-designed storage zones for coats, shoes, bags, and seasonal items. The key is creating designated spaces that are both functional and durable enough to handle daily use.

Comprehensive Construction Process

Let's walk through the detailed process of creating effective mudroom storage units:

1. Space Analysis and Planning
Begin with thorough space evaluation:

Traffic Flow Assessment:
- Analyze entry and exit patterns

- Measure doorway clearances
- Consider traffic bottlenecks
- Plan for multiple users
- Account for seasonal changes
- Map natural movement paths

Storage Requirements:
- List items needing storage
- Measure typical coat lengths
- Consider boot and shoe sizes
- Plan for sports equipment
- Account for seasonal gear
- Include space for growth

2. Design Development
Create a functional layout that serves all users:

Unit Configuration:
- Design individual storage zones
- Plan bench height and depth
- Calculate hook placement heights
- Design shelf spacing
- Include shoe storage
- Create charging stations

Material Selection:
- Choose durable flooring materials
- Select moisture-resistant finishes
- Pick appropriate hardware
- Plan ventilation features
- Consider easy-clean surfaces
- Select robust construction materials

3. Construction Implementation
Build systematically for durability:

Base Construction:
- Install level foundation
- Build sturdy framework
- Add moisture barriers
- Create proper drainage
- Install flooring system
- Ensure solid anchoring

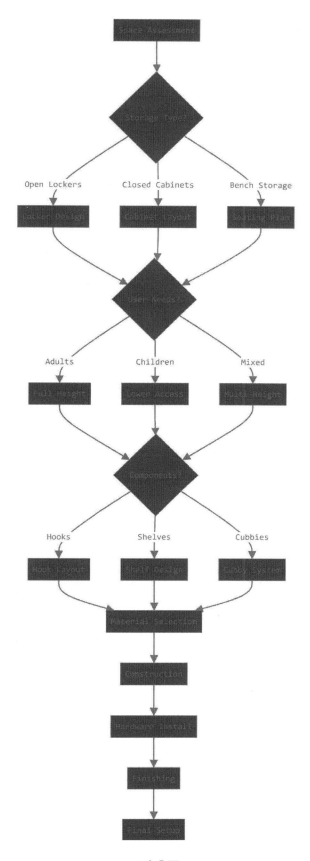

Mudroom Storage Design Guide

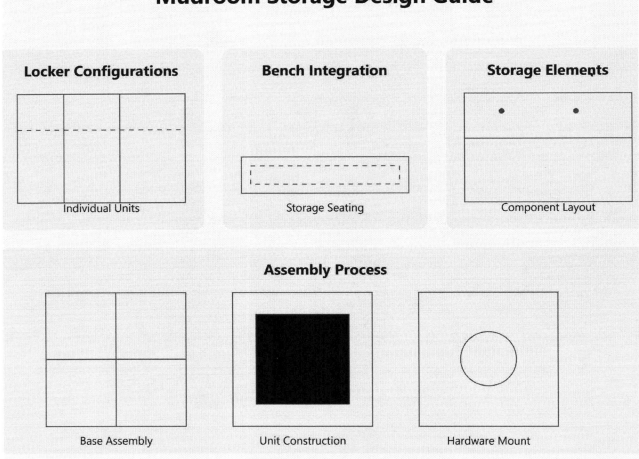

Locker Configurations

Individual Units

Bench Integration

Storage Seating

Storage Elements

Component Layout

Assembly Process

Base Assembly

Unit Construction

Hardware Mount

Under-Stairs Storage Solutions

]Let me guide you through the process of creating efficient under-stairs storage solutions. Think of the space under your stairs as a puzzle – like a tetris game where each piece of available space needs to be thoughtfully utilized. Just as a ship's cabin makes use of every nook and cranny, under-stairs storage requires creative thinking to maximize irregular spaces.

Understanding Under-Stairs Space Utilization

Before we begin construction, we need to understand how stairs create unique storage opportunities. Imagine your staircase as a series of incrementally changing spaces – the area closest to the steps creates triangular pockets of storage potential, while the taller spaces beneath can accommodate larger items.

Detailed Implementation Process

Let me walk you through the comprehensive process of creating under-stairs storage:

1. Space Analysis and Planning
Begin with careful measurement and assessment:

Dimensional Analysis:
- Measure total available height
- Calculate depth at various points
- Document stair angle precisely
- Note structural elements
- Identify utility locations
- Check floor level variations

Access Assessment:
- Evaluate approach angles
- Consider door swing space
- Plan traffic patterns
- Account for headroom
- Check lighting requirements
- Note ventilation needs

2. Design Development
Create a storage solution that maximizes space:

Zone Planning:
- Divide space by height segments
- Plan storage types by zone
- Design access methods
- Account for irregular shapes
- Include proper clearances
- Plan lighting integration

Storage Configuration:
- Design drawer depths
- Plan door sizes
- Calculate shelf spacing
- Include adjustable elements
- Design specialty storage
- Plan for future flexibility

3. Construction Implementation
Build systematically for maximum efficiency:

Framework Construction:
- Install level base supports
- Build vertical frame members
- Add horizontal supports
- Create division framework
- Ensure proper bracing
- Verify square and plumb

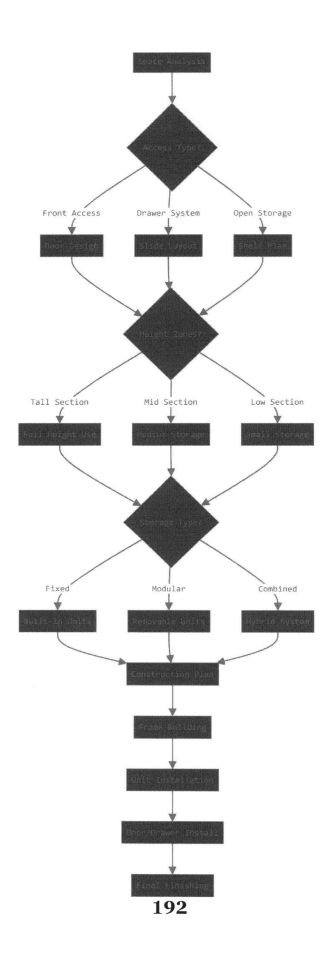

192

Under-Stairs Storage Guide

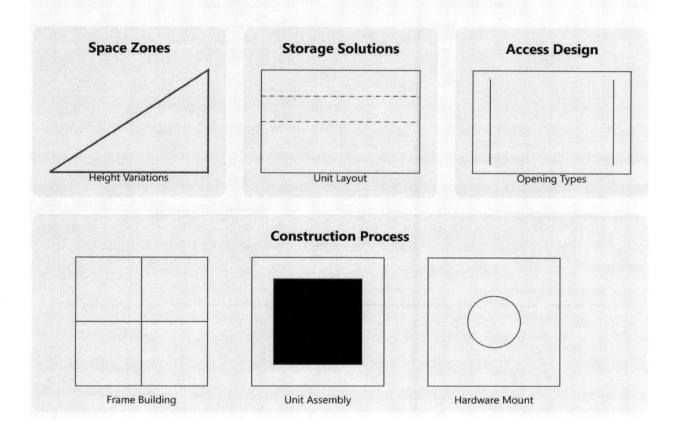

Space Zones

Height Variations

Storage Solutions

Unit Layout

Access Design

Opening Types

Construction Process

Frame Building

Unit Assembly

Hardware Mount

Chapter 9
Special Techniques and Finishing

Edge Banding and Trim Work

Let me guide you through the detailed process of edge banding and trim work, essential techniques that transform raw edges into polished, professional finishes. Think of edge banding as the frame around a painting - just as a frame completes and protects artwork, edge banding and trim finish and protect exposed edges while enhancing the overall appearance of your project.

Understanding Edge Treatment Fundamentals

Before applying any edge treatment, we must understand how different materials and methods work together. Consider how a tailor finishes the edges of fine garments - different materials and situations call for different finishing techniques. Similarly, woodworking edge treatments must be matched to both the material and the project's requirements.

Systematic Application Process

Let me walk you through the detailed process of applying edge banding and trim:

1. Surface Preparation

Proper preparation is crucial for successful edge banding:

Edge Preparation:
- Clean edges thoroughly
- Sand to ensure smoothness
- Remove all dust
- Check for damage
- Ensure straight edges
- Verify square corners

Material Preparation:
- Cut banding slightly oversized
- Check adhesive type
- Prepare application tools
- Set up work surface
- Organize materials
- Test temperature settings

2. Application Process

Apply edge banding with careful attention to detail:

For Iron-On Banding:
- Set iron temperature correctly
- Position banding carefully
- Apply steady pressure
- Move at consistent speed
- Check for full adhesion

- Allow proper cooling

For Pre-Glued Banding:
- Apply contact cement evenly
- Allow proper tacking time
- Position carefully
- Roll firmly
- Check for bubbles
- Ensure full contact

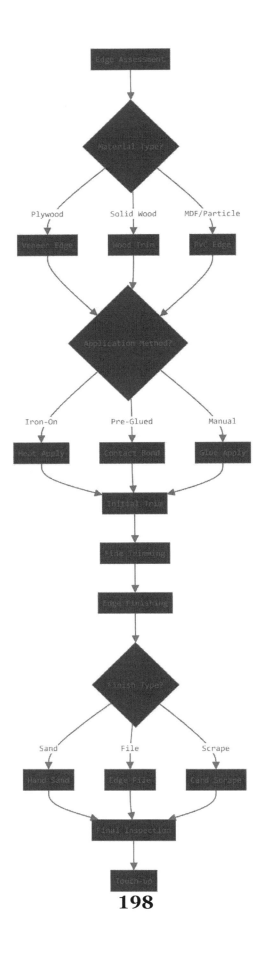

198

Edge Banding Techniques

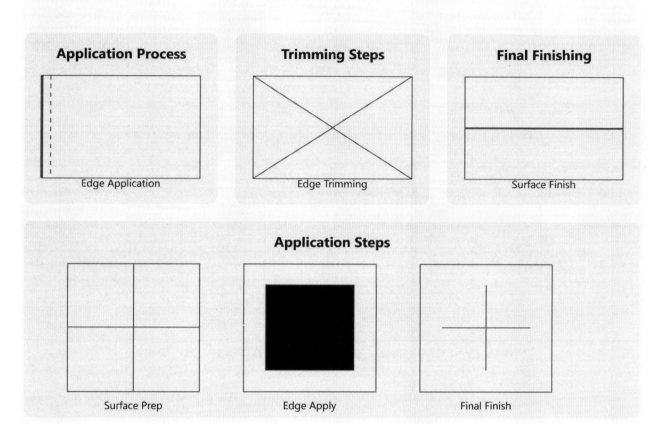

Application Process

Edge Application

Trimming Steps

Edge Trimming

Final Finishing

Surface Finish

Application Steps

Surface Prep

Edge Apply

Final Finish

Surface Preparation

Let me guide you through the essential process of surface preparation, which is truly the cornerstone of any successful woodworking project. Think of surface preparation like preparing a canvas for a masterpiece painting - just as an artist needs a properly prepared surface to create their best work, woodworkers need properly prepared surfaces to achieve professional results.

Understanding Surface Preparation Fundamentals

Before we begin working on any surface, we need to understand how wood responds to different preparation techniques. Consider how a piece of wood is like a landscape with hills and valleys at the microscopic level. Our goal is to systematically level these variations while maintaining the wood's natural beauty and structural integrity.

Comprehensive Surface Preparation Process

Let me walk you through the detailed process of preparing surfaces for finishing:

1. Initial Assessment
Begin with careful evaluation of the surface:

Surface Investigation:
- Examine under good lighting
- Feel for irregularities
- Note grain direction
- Identify problem areas
- Check for damage
- Document repairs needed

Environmental Preparation:
- Set up proper lighting
- Ensure good ventilation
- Organize tools needed
- Prepare work surface
- Gather safety equipment
- Set up dust collection

2. Progressive Surface Preparation
Follow a systematic approach:

For Raw Wood:
- Begin with appropriate grit
- Work with the grain
- Progress through grits methodically
- Check surface frequently
- Remove dust between grits
- Maintain consistent pressure

For Repairs:
- Clean damaged areas thoroughly
- Apply appropriate filler
- Allow proper drying time
- Sand carefully to blend
- Check for matching texture
- Verify repair stability

3. Quality Control Process
Maintain high standards throughout:

Visual Inspection:
- Use raking light technique
- Check at different angles
- Look for scratch patterns
- Verify consistent texture
- Examine edges carefully
- Document problem areas

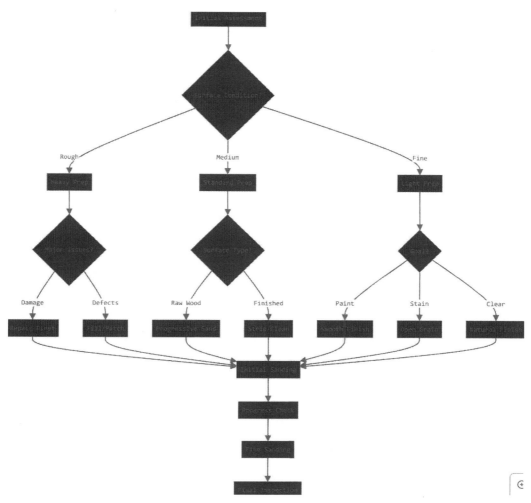

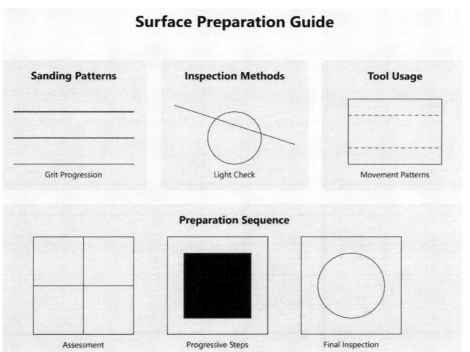

Surface Preparation Guide

Sanding Patterns

Grit Progression

Inspection Methods

Light Check

Tool Usage

Movement Patterns

Preparation Sequence

Assessment

Progressive Steps

Final Inspection

203

Finishing Techniques for Storage Projects

Let me guide you through the comprehensive process of finishing storage projects. Think of finishing as both armor and beautification for your woodwork - just as a car needs both paint for protection and polish for aesthetics, your storage pieces need finishes that both protect and enhance their appearance.

Understanding Finishing Requirements for Storage

Storage pieces face unique finishing challenges because they experience frequent handling, potential moisture exposure, and varying environmental conditions. Like designing a protective coating for frequently used tools, we need to create finishes that can withstand daily use while maintaining their beauty.

Detailed Finishing Process

Let me walk you through the comprehensive process of finishing storage projects:

1. Environment and Use Assessment
Begin by understanding the project's requirements:

Usage Evaluation:
- Determine frequency of handling
- Assess moisture exposure risk
- Consider UV light exposure
- Evaluate temperature variations
- Note cleaning requirements
- Plan for wear patterns

Environmental Factors:
- Measure ambient humidity
- Check temperature stability
- Consider ventilation needs
- Plan dust control
- Evaluate lighting conditions
- Account for seasonal changes

2. Finish Selection
Choose appropriate products:

For High-Use Areas:
- Select durable finishes
- Consider water resistance
- Plan multiple protective layers
- Use appropriate sealers
- Choose suitable hardeners
- Test on sample pieces

For Decorative Surfaces:
- Select enhancing finishes
- Consider grain highlighting
- Plan color development
- Choose appropriate sheens
- Test finish combinations
- Verify aesthetic goals

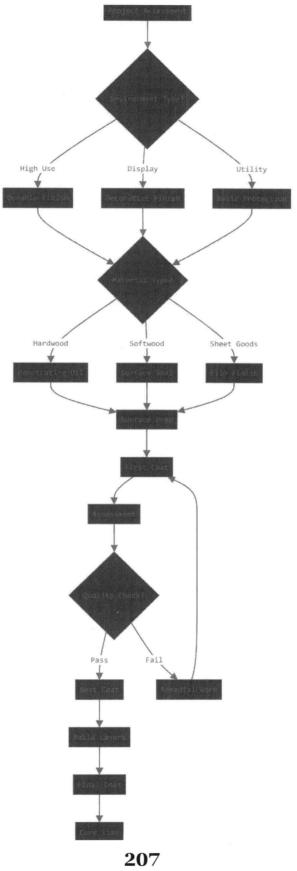

Finishing Techniques Guide

Application Techniques

Stroke Patterns

Layer Development

Build-up Process

Surface Treatment

Treatment Methods

Finishing Process

Surface Preparation

Finish Application

Final Treatment

Hardware Installation and Adjustment

Let me guide you through the precise process of hardware installation and adjustment, a critical skill that determines how well your storage pieces will function. Think of hardware like the joints in a dancer's body - just as a dancer needs properly tuned joints for graceful movement, your cabinets and storage units need correctly installed and adjusted hardware for smooth, reliable operation.

Understanding Hardware Installation Fundamentals

Before we begin any installation, we need to understand how different types of hardware work together to create smooth operation. Consider each piece of hardware as part of an orchestrated system - like musicians in an orchestra, each component must be perfectly tuned and positioned to create harmony in operation.

Comprehensive Installation Process

Let me guide you through the detailed process of installing and adjusting hardware:

1. Pre-Installation Planning
Begin with thorough preparation:

Layout Development:
- Review hardware specifications
- Create installation templates
- Mark mounting locations
- Verify clearances
- Check reveal requirements
- Plan adjustment access

Tool Preparation:
- Gather required tools
- Prepare drill guides
- Select appropriate bits
- Set up power tools
- Organize hardware sets
- Prepare work surface

2. Installation Sequence
Follow a systematic approach:

For Hinge Installation:
- Mark hinge locations precisely
- Create mortises if needed
- Pre-drill mounting holes
- Mount cabinet plates
- Attach door components
- Test initial fit

For Drawer Slides:
- Mark slide locations
- Verify drawer clearances
- Mount cabinet members
- Install drawer members
- Check smooth operation
- Make initial adjustments

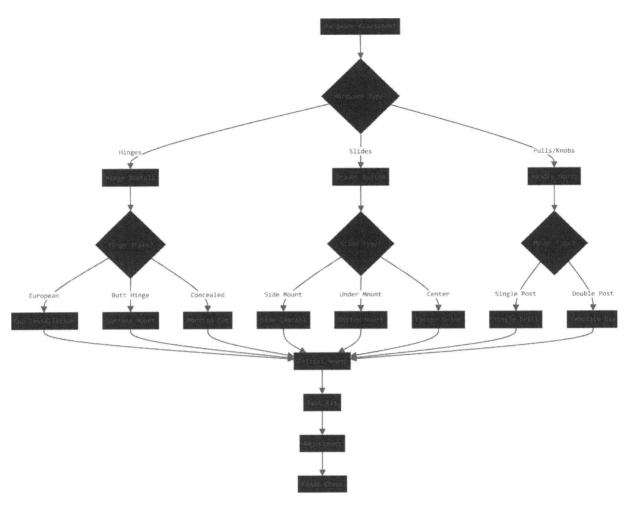

Hardware Installation Guide

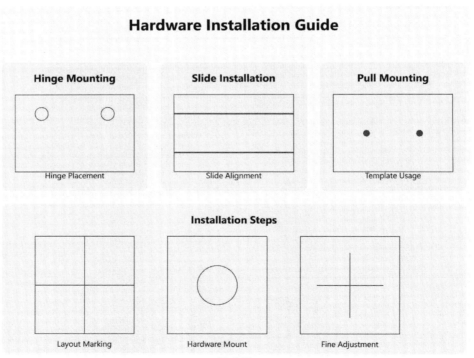

Hinge Mounting

Hinge Placement

Slide Installation

Slide Alignment

Pull Mounting

Template Usage

Installation Steps

Layout Marking

Hardware Mount

Fine Adjustment

PART IV
TIPS AND
TROUBLESHOOTING

Chapter 10
Problem-Solving Guide

Common Construction Challenges

Let me guide you through a comprehensive approach to handling common construction challenges in storage projects. Think of this as creating a diagnostic manual for woodworking - just as a doctor uses systematic methods to identify and treat medical conditions, we need organized approaches to identify and resolve construction issues.

Understanding Problem-Solving Fundamentals

Before diving into specific solutions, we need to understand how construction problems develop. Like a detective investigating a case, we need to look for clues, understand cause-and-effect relationships, and develop systematic approaches to resolution.

Systematic Problem-Solving Process

Let me walk you through the detailed process of addressing common construction challenges:

1. Problem Identification
Begin with careful observation and analysis:

Visual Assessment:
- Examine the issue carefully
- Note specific symptoms
- Document problem areas
- Look for patterns
- Consider timing of issues
- Check surrounding areas

Physical Testing:
- Test joint movement
- Check for square
- Verify dimensions
- Assess stability
- Test operation
- Measure tolerances

2. Root Cause Analysis
Determine the underlying issue:

For Joint Problems:
- Check wood movement
- Verify joint fit
- Examine glue lines
- Test joint strength
- Look for stress points
- Assess alignment

For Material Issues:
- Evaluate moisture content
- Check grain orientation
- Look for defects
- Assess wood quality
- Consider environmental factors
- Test material stability

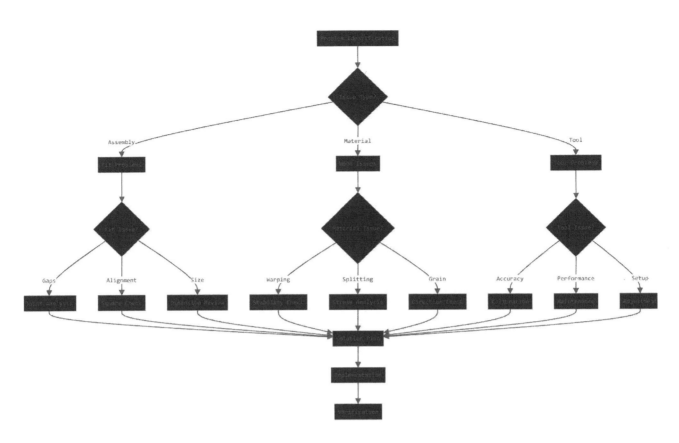

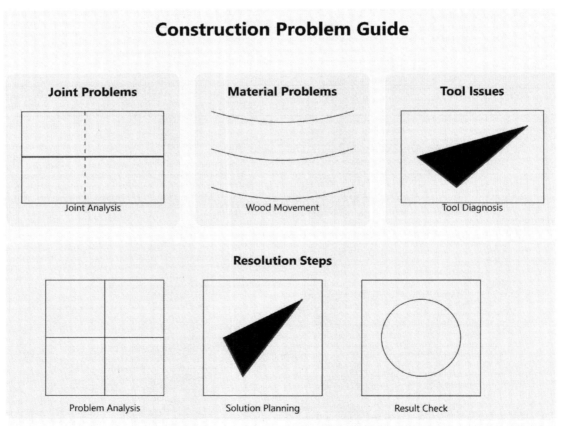

Construction Problem Guide

Joint Problems

Joint Analysis

Material Problems

Wood Movement

Tool Issues

Tool Diagnosis

Resolution Steps

Problem Analysis

Solution Planning

Result Check

Fixing Alignment Issues

Let me guide you through the intricate process of resolving alignment issues in storage projects. Think of alignment like tuning a piano - just as each string must be precisely adjusted to create harmony, each component of your project must be perfectly aligned for proper function and appearance.

Understanding Alignment Fundamentals

Before we tackle alignment corrections, we need to understand how different components relate to each other in three-dimensional space. Imagine your project as a building - just as a building needs to be level, plumb, and square, your storage pieces need perfect alignment in multiple planes.

Systematic Alignment Correction Process

Let me walk you through the detailed process of fixing alignment issues:

1. Assessment Phase
Begin with thorough evaluation:

Measurement Process:
- Check all reveals
- Measure diagonals

- Verify level conditions
- Test operation
- Document current state
- Identify reference points

Visual Analysis:
- Look for binding points
- Check gap consistency
- Observe movement patterns
- Note wear patterns
- Assess hardware function
- Review overall appearance

2. Correction Implementation
Follow a systematic approach:

For Door Alignment:
- Adjust hinge positions
- Modify mounting plates
- Check door stability
- Verify clearances
- Test swing operation
- Fine-tune reveals

For Drawer Alignment:
- Level slide mounts
- Adjust drawer fronts
- Check slide function

- Verify drawer box square
- Test smooth operation
- Fine-tune clearances

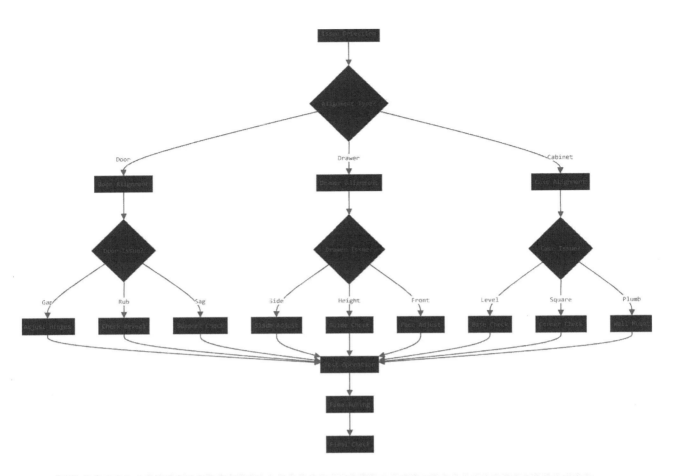

Alignment Correction Guide

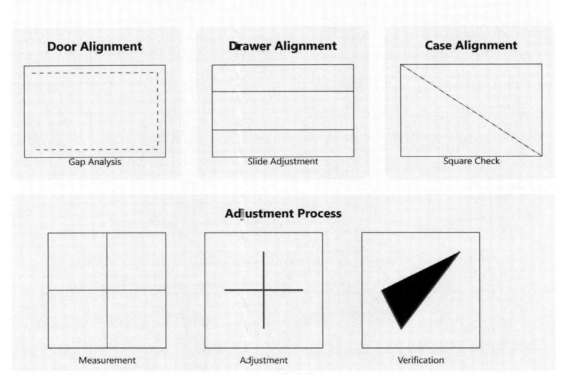

Door Alignment

Gap Analysis

Drawer Alignment

Slide Adjustment

Case Alignment

Square Check

Adjustment Process

Measurement

Adjustment

Verification

Dealing with Wood Movement

Let me guide you through the intricacies of dealing with wood movement in storage projects. Think of wood as a living, breathing material that continues to respond to its environment long after the tree is harvested. Just as our skin expands and contracts with temperature and moisture, wood fibers react to environmental changes in predictable but important ways.

Understanding Wood Movement Fundamentals

Before we can effectively manage wood movement, we need to understand how wood behaves at a cellular level. Imagine wood cells as bundles of straws - they can absorb and release moisture, causing them to swell and shrink. This movement happens primarily across the grain, while movement along the grain is minimal.

Managing Wood Movement: Step-by-Step Process

Let me walk you through the systematic approach to managing wood movement:

1. Assessment Phase
Begin with thorough material evaluation:

Wood Analysis:
- Identify wood species
- Determine grain orientation
- Calculate movement potential
- Consider seasonal changes
- Check moisture content
- Note current conditions

Environmental Factors:
- Measure ambient humidity
- Track temperature variations
- Assess air circulation
- Consider seasonal changes
- Document location conditions
- Plan for extremes

2. Design Accommodation
Plan for inevitable movement:

Panel Construction:
- Calculate expansion space
- Design floating panels
- Size groove depth
- Plan panel alignment
- Include movement gaps
- Design proper supports

Frame Construction:
- Choose appropriate joints
- Size mortise and tenons
- Plan rail orientation
- Consider grain direction
- Design corner blocks
- Include expansion gaps

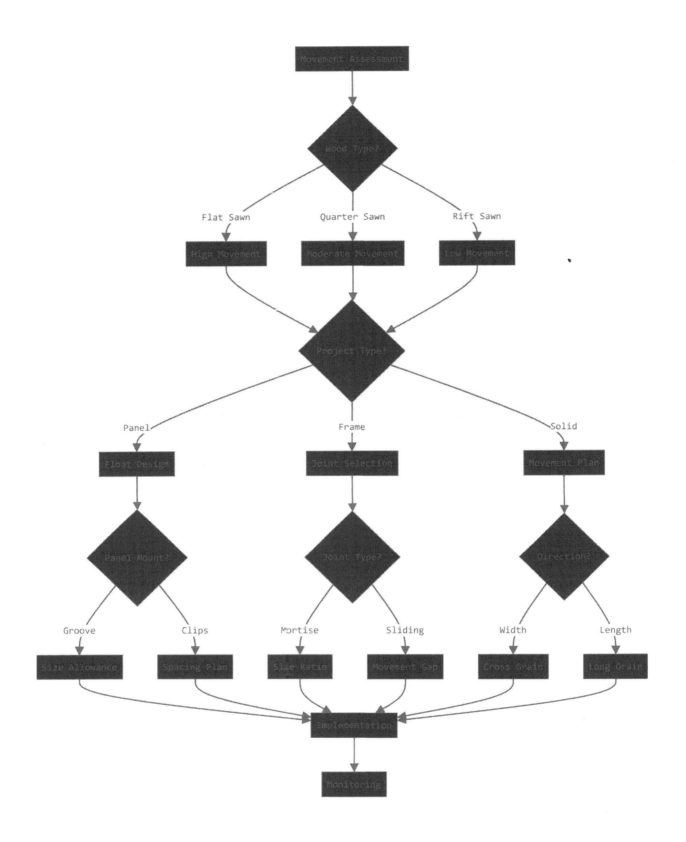

Wood Movement Guide

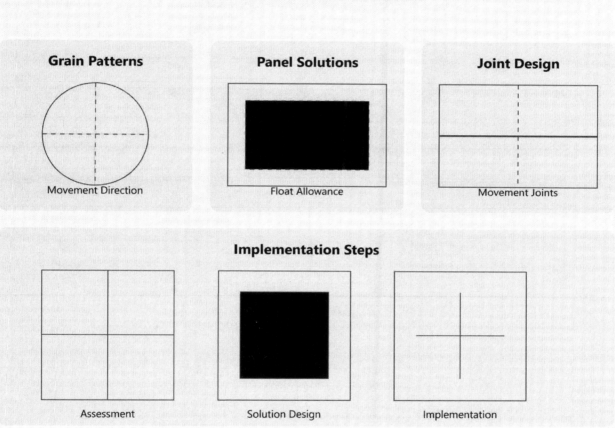

Grain Patterns

Movement Direction

Panel Solutions

Float Allowance

Joint Design

Movement Joints

Implementation Steps

Assessment

Solution Design

Implementation

Maintenance and Repairs

Let me guide you through the essential process of maintaining and repairing storage projects. Think of your storage pieces like a car - just as vehicles need regular maintenance and occasional repairs to perform reliably, your cabinets, drawers, and storage units require consistent care and timely repairs to maintain their functionality and appearance over the years.

Understanding Maintenance Fundamentals

Before we dive into specific procedures, let's understand how regular maintenance prevents major issues. Consider maintenance like preventive healthcare - regular checkups and minor interventions can prevent serious problems from developing, while proper repair techniques ensure long-term solutions rather than temporary fixes.

Systematic Maintenance Process

Let me walk you through the comprehensive approach to maintenance and repairs:

1. Regular Inspection Schedule
Establish a routine inspection system:

Visual Inspection:
- Check all joints regularly
- Examine finish condition
- Inspect hardware function
- Look for wear patterns
- Monitor wood movement
- Document changes

Operational Testing:
- Test drawer operation
- Check door alignment
- Verify smooth movement
- Listen for unusual sounds
- Feel for resistance
- Note any changes

2. Preventive Maintenance
Implement regular care procedures:

Hardware Care:
- Clean sliding mechanisms
- Lubricate moving parts
- Tighten loose fasteners
- Check alignment
- Test adjustments
- Document maintenance

Surface Maintenance:
- Clean surfaces properly
- Apply appropriate treatments
- Protect from damage
- Monitor humidity effects
- Address minor issues
- Maintain protective finishes

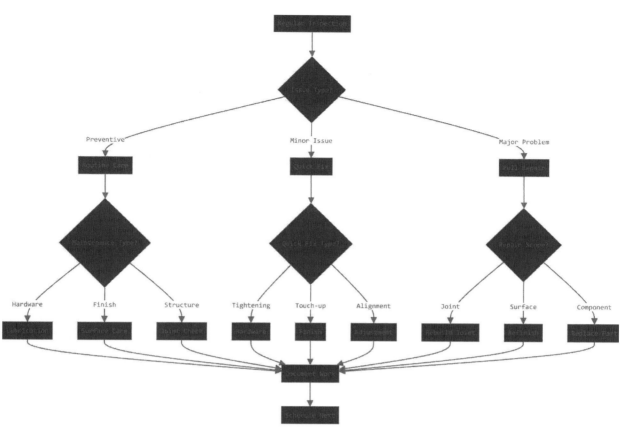

Maintenance Guide

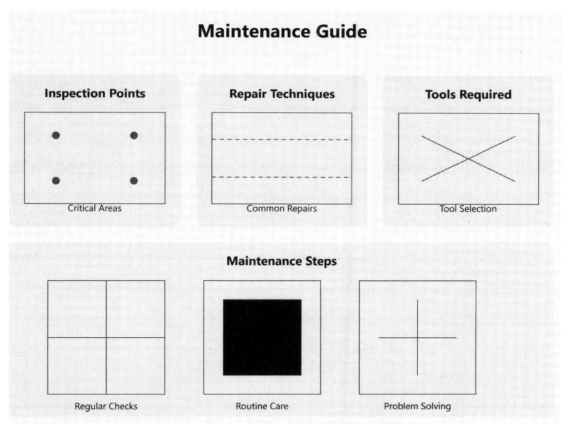

Inspection Points	Repair Techniques	Tools Required
Critical Areas	Common Repairs	Tool Selection

Maintenance Steps

Regular Checks	Routine Care	Problem Solving

Appendix A

Cut Lists and Materials Guide

Let me guide you through the essential process of creating and using cut lists, as well as understanding materials selection for your storage projects. Think of a cut list as your project's recipe - just as a chef needs precise measurements of ingredients before cooking, a woodworker needs exact dimensions and quantities before making the first cut.

The Foundation of Cut Lists

A cut list serves three critical purposes:
1. Material Optimization - It helps minimize waste by planning the most efficient use of your materials
2. Project Organization - It provides a clear roadmap of all components needed
3. Cost Estimation - It allows accurate calculation of material costs before beginning

Let me explain how to develop a proper cut list that will serve these purposes effectively.

Creating a Comprehensive Cut List

First, let's understand the essential elements every cut list should include:

For each component, you need to document:
- Final dimensions (length $\times$ width $\times$ thickness)
- Grain direction requirements
- Material type and grade
- Quantity needed
- Purpose or location in the project
- Any special notes about joinery or edge treatment

For example, if you're building a cabinet, your cut list might include:

```

Cabinet Side (2 pieces)
- 30" $\times$ 24" $\times$ 3/4" Cherry plywood
- Grain running vertical
- Edge banding on front edge
- Dado for bottom panel at 4" from bottom

Cabinet Top/Bottom (2 pieces)
- 24" $\times$ 23-1/4" $\times$ 3/4" Cherry plywood
- Grain running front to back
- Edge banding on front edge only
```

Material Selection Guidelines

When selecting materials, consider these key factors:

Wood Selection:
- Project requirements (structural vs decorative)
- Environmental conditions (humidity, temperature variations)
- Budget constraints
- Aesthetic preferences
- Availability of materials
- Finishing requirements

For plywood projects:
- Grade of plywood (cabinet grade vs construction grade)
- Core type (void-free vs standard)
- Veneer thickness
- Number of plies
- Face veneer species match

Calculating Material Requirements

To determine total material needs:
1. Add up all similar components
2. Group by material type
3. Add waste factor (typically 15-20% for solid wood, 10% for sheet goods)

4. Consider grain matching requirements

5. Account for test pieces and mistakes

For example, if your project needs:
- 4 pieces at 24" length
- 2 pieces at 36" length
- Add 15% waste factor

Total length needed $= (4 \times 24") + (2 \times 36") = 168" +$ waste $= 193"$ or approximately 17 linear feet

Advanced Planning Considerations

For optimal material usage:

Sheet Goods Planning:
- Create cutting diagrams
- Consider grain direction
- Plan for efficient cuts
- Leave room for saw kerfs
- Account for trimming edges
- Plan cuts to minimize waste

Solid Wood Planning:
- Account for wood movement
- Plan for grain matching
- Consider wood stability
- Allow for milling waste **234**

- Plan for joinery requirements

Pro Tips for Material Efficiency

1. Purchase Materials Strategically:
   - Buy slightly oversized for flexibility
   - Select straight, stable boards
   - Check moisture content
   - Verify grade and quality
   - Inspect for defects

2. Optimize Cutting Sequence:
   - Cut longest pieces first
   - Group similar cuts together
   - Save offcuts for smaller pieces
   - Label pieces clearly
   - Maintain organized workspace

Appendix B

Hardware Selection Guide

Let me guide you through the detailed process of selecting appropriate hardware for your storage projects. Think of hardware as the joints and muscles of your project - just like our bodies need the right ligaments and tendons to move properly, your storage pieces need the right hardware to function effectively and reliably.

Understanding Hardware Categories

Hardware can be divided into several fundamental categories, each serving specific functions:

1. Movement Hardware
Movement hardware allows components to operate smoothly and reliably. Consider drawer slides, for instance. Just as we choose different shoes for different activities, we select different slides based on usage requirements:

Ball-Bearing Slides:
- Offer smooth operation under heavy loads
- Typically rated for 75-100 pounds
- Available in various extension lengths
- Provide consistent performance

- Work well for frequently used drawers
- More expensive but highly durable

Undermount Slides:
- Create clean look with hidden mechanism
- Often include soft-close features
- Support moderate to heavy loads
- Require precise installation
- Excellent for kitchen and bath applications
- Premium price point justified by features

2. Mounting Hardware

Mounting hardware secures components together and to walls. Like the foundation of a building, these components must be chosen carefully:

Cabinet Hinges:
European Style:
- Offer multiple adjustments
- Hidden when door is closed
- Support various door thicknesses
- Include soft-close options
- Require precise boring
- Available in different overlays

Traditional Hinges:
- Provide decorative options

- Simpler installation process
- Limited adjustment capability
- Visible when door is closed
- More forgiving of installation variances
- Often less expensive

3. Organizational Hardware
These components enhance functionality:

Pull-Out Systems:
- Maximize corner space usage
- Improve accessibility
- Various configurations available
- Weight ratings critical
- Consider clearance requirements
- Installation complexity varies

Selection Criteria

When choosing hardware, consider these key factors:

Usage Intensity:
- Frequency of operation
- Expected load requirements
- User demographics
- Environmental conditions
- Maintenance requirements
- Life expectancy

Installation Requirements:
- Tool availability
- Skill level needed
- Space constraints
- Adjustment needs
- Mounting surface compatibility
- Access for maintenance

Cost Considerations:
- Initial purchase price
- Installation time/cost
- Long-term durability
- Replacement availability
- Warranty coverage
- Upgrade potential

Hardware Specifications Guide

For accurate selection, understand these specifications:

Drawer Slides:
- Load rating (pounds/kilograms)
- Extension length (partial/full/over)
- Side clearance requirements
- Length options available
- Movement type (roller/ball bearing)
- Special features (soft-close, push-to-open)

Hinges:
- Door thickness range
- Overlay requirements
- Opening angle
- Adjustment ranges
- Mounting style
- Weight capacity

Glossary

Let me help you understand the essential terminology used in storage and cabinet making projects. Think of this glossary as your woodworking translator - just as learning a new language opens up understanding, knowing these terms helps you better comprehend and communicate about woodworking projects.

A

Allowance
The extra space or material included in measurements to account for wood movement, fitting, or finishing. For example, when making a drawer, we include an allowance of about 1/16" on each side for smooth operation.

Assembly
The process of joining individual components to create the final piece. Like putting together a puzzle, assembly requires careful attention to the order of operations and proper alignment of parts.

B

Biscuit Joint

A woodworking joint that uses a small, football-shaped piece of compressed wood (the biscuit) inserted into matching slots in two pieces of wood. Similar to how a dowel joins pieces together, but with a flat oval shape instead of a round one.

Blocking

Supporting pieces of wood added to strengthen a joint or provide additional mounting surfaces. Think of blocking like the studs in a wall - they provide crucial support behind the visible surface.

C

Case

The main body or framework of a cabinet or storage unit. Like the walls of a house, the case provides the primary structure and support for all other components.

Counterbore

A wider, flat-bottomed hole drilled at the surface of the wood to allow a screw head to sit below the surface. Imagine creating a small pocket for the screw head to nest into.

D

Dado

A groove cut across the grain of a piece of wood to accept another piece. Like creating a small channel for a shelf to sit in, providing both support and alignment.

Dovetail

A strong woodworking joint resembling the shape of a dove's tail, used particularly in drawer construction. The interlocking fingers provide both strength and decorative appeal.

E

Edge Banding

A thin strip of material applied to the exposed edges of plywood or other sheet goods to cover the core material. Think of it as trim that creates a finished look while protecting the edge.

Expansion Gap

Space left around panels or boards to allow for natural wood movement with changes in humidity. Like leaving room for thermal expansion in bridge construction, these gaps prevent warping and splitting.

F

Face Frame
The frame attached to the front of a cabinet case, providing strength and a mounting surface for doors and drawers. Similar to a picture frame, it frames the cabinet opening while adding structural support.

Flush
When two surfaces are even with each other, neither protruding nor recessed. Like a well-fitted door that sits perfectly even with its frame.

G

Grain
The direction and pattern of wood fibers in a piece of lumber. Understanding grain direction is crucial for both strength and appearance, like understanding the weave in fabric.

Guide
A component that directs the movement of a drawer or sliding part. Think of guides like train tracks, keeping movement smooth and controlled.

Made in the USA
Columbia, SC
09 June 2025

5350ed2f-6cfe-418d-8a80-8aad92f38b5eR01